LONELINESS
IN THE SCHOOLS
(What to do about it)

LONELINESS

IN THE SCHOOLS

(What to do about it)

Marc Robert, Ed. D.

ARGUS COMMUNICATIONS

Niles, Illinois

Argus Communications
7440 Natchez Avenue
Niles, Illinois 60648

International Standard Book Number: 0-913592-18-8
Library of Congress Catalog Card Number: 73-78537

To Tracy, Matthew and Amy
who helped me better understand
the process of "schooling" . . .

CONTENTS

FOREWORD

I wholeheartedly recommend **Loneliness in the Schools** as "must" reading for anyone involved or interested in education. Dr. Marc Robert is an educator with whom I have worked personally for eight years. During this time, I saw him apply his educational experience and competence to solve the knotty problem of how to run a school where students really learn and feel good about themselves and others.

In this book, Marc Robert details in an easy-to-read, honest style what he does to create successful learning environments. **Loneliness in the Schools** not only will tell you what you can do as a teacher, administrator, or parent to improve the quality of your educational institution, but it also will make you **want** to do it. This volume can make the difference between students' experiencing success or failure in school.

Since children must go to school and since many schools are lonely places where there is too much failure, it is crucial to listen to a man who has proved himself in the field. Students will **want** to go to the kind of school Dr. Robert works to develop.

Many books tell us what we're doing wrong in the schools. Here is a book that tells us what we can do right—by a man who did it right. Read it to see how it is done, and learn. I did.

William Glasser, M.D.

INTRODUCTION

Since the early 1960's, scholars and romantics alike increasingly have focused on educational problems and have proposed all kinds of solutions. Despite the volume of their criticisms and plans, very little significant change has taken place, primarily because planners for improving education have not considered what is happening to people in the schools day by day and minute by minute.

In our preoccupation with broad programs and systems, we have ignored the need for human interaction within the schools and the personal needs of the students and teachers who live there from four to ten hours a day, five days a week, during the school year.

During the more than twenty years I have spent working as a teacher and administrator in the Los Angeles school system, I have observed a growing alienation of the individuals within the school community. They are becoming estranged one from the other—students moving away from students, teachers from students, teachers from teachers, teachers from principals, teachers and principals from higher administration, and school staffs from their local communities. These separations are manifest in declining teacher and student morale, lower academic achievement, vandalism, increased staff militancy, and community-school conflict. Specific and practical methods are needed to counteract the growing separation and resultant loneliness of people in the schools. This book is meant to be used as an aid in meeting that need. *Although most of what I have to say pertains to the elementary school, much of it is applicable to high schools.*

One often gets the eerie impression of huge clouds of educational reform drifting back and forth from coast to coast and only occasionally touching down to blanket an actual educational institution.
National Education Association Journal.

A Note to the Reader

This is not a textbook. It is a self-help action motivator, designed to bring people in the schools together for the purpose of reducing their common loneliness. It will be useful only if it is shared, discussed and applied.

Part I was written to help readers examine what is wrong with schools in which students and staff members are uninvolved and lonely. Chapters 1 through 5 identify specific loneliness-causing factors which interfere with the effectiveness of people working and learning in the schools. These factors were described to me repeatedly by hundreds of teachers and administrators with whom I worked.

As you read through these chapters, ask yourself if any of the conditions described are separating the people in your school. If so, to what extent? Which separators are the most detrimental to personal and professional relationships? Are there other factors not mentioned in these chapters? Use the planning sheets at the ends of Chapters 1 through 5 to help assess the human relationships existing in your school.

Part II offers suggestions for bringing staff members and students together in ways calculated to counteract the separation factors discussed in Part I. Whether these ideas are implemented is not nearly as important as whether readers are stimulated to search out and develop ways of coping with their specific school loneliness problems.

Questions for your consideration and action are at the end of of each section in Chapters 6 and 7. Test your opinions against them individually, in discussion groups, or during staff meetings.

Finally, begin making some concrete plans to reduce or eliminate some of the separators in your school—either by applying some of the ideas in this book or by developing better ones of your own.

PART I

CHAPTER ONE

WHAT CAUSES LONELINESS IN THE SCHOOLS?

4

Many programs have been directed toward re-involving alienated and underachieving students in the educational environment, yet little attention has been given to the problem of the lonely and alienated teacher and principal. Since students are directly affected by the actions and attitudes modeled by their teachers, efforts must be made to create environments that enable teachers to achieve professional satisfaction, which I believe is the key factor in improving education. *Teachers who do not achieve professional self-worth suffer a type of loneliness and pain that may influence from thirty to one hundred and fifty students each day.*

Professional loneliness can be defined as the feeling experienced by teachers that no one cares about them or what they do in the school; that they are not really important or influential; that they are just expected to hold the lid on; that the expedient course of action is the way to survive. These feelings, grounded in a lack of psychic support, are manifest in many ways.

Teacher Anxieties

Caused by not knowing what to expect next from "above." What new program, accountability demand, or additional workload will be added or required this year? The result of these anxieties is a growing resistance to change and a dogged defense of the status quo.

Teacher Antagonisms

Caused by poor communication and misunderstanding. As a result, many teachers assume an adversary attitude and set themselves against the administration, the students and the parents.

Teacher Absenteeism and Resignations

Caused by the feeling that they are not quite making it even though they are trying hard and doing their best. They also feel that there is no one to talk with about their problems.

Teacher Fears

Caused by believing that if they make a mistake, there will be conflict either with parents or the administration, and they will be vulnerable and without support.

Any teacher can from his own experience add many more frustrations and "gut" reactions to the list of attitudes that cause discomfort and desperation. Although staff members in many school systems are exerting efforts to overcome the dehumanizing forces at work in the schools, the factors which contribute to separation and loneliness seem to be growing ever stronger.

For nearly two years I have had the opportunity of talking at length with teachers and principals in many parts of the United States. This was one of my responsibilities in conducting Schools Without Failure Seminars.[1] The teachers are remarkably consistent in what they are saying about their professional satisfaction or lack of it. Whether in California, Kansas, Florida, New Mexico, or Pennsylvania, many teachers feel that *the school environment keeps them and the students uninvolved and lonely.*

Most teachers do not have a chance to talk regularly with their colleagues about matters of professional interest. They find themselves in separate classrooms doing their own thing. They feel that the school is a collection of classrooms instead of an educational institution made up of people who have a common purpose. This point was impressed upon me dramatically when I recently telephoned a fellow principal who had been transferred to an inner-city school in Los Angeles. During our conversation, I

---

[1] Schools Without Failure Seminars are college classes conducted at school sites under the auspices of the Educator Training Center in Los Angeles, California and La Verne College, La Verne, California. These classes emphasize practical application of the ideas in Dr. William Glasser's book, *Schools Without Failure* (New York: Harper & Row, 1969).

Teacher anxieties

asked him what was the best thing that happened to him since his reassignment. He replied without hesitation, "The '71 earthquake." Perplexed, I asked him what he meant. He explained. "The day after the earthquake the kids stayed home for a day, and the teachers and I talked about school. We needed to communicate so much that we talked on and on. I think that one day will sustain us for the rest of the year." Here was an extremely competent and well-thought-of principal saying that it took a disaster to enable his staff to discuss and plan together for their school.

This lack of communication breeds a feeling of professional loneliness. There is a very limited amount of positive contact between teachers and administrators. Teachers in large schools sometimes wait for a week to talk with a principal about a problem or an idea. The principal is drowned in paper work, overwhelmed with meetings, and faced with one crisis after another. This leaves him feeling guilty about his limited contact with the staff. Because of lack of time to communicate, misunderstandings develop. The resultant frustration and disappointment often cause teachers to withdraw into lonely classrooms and to develop a what's-the-use attitude, while the principal is forced into becoming an adversary instead of a helper.

Teachers with whom I worked indicated another factor standing in the way of professional satisfaction. They felt that during the past ten or fifteen years students have changed. They tend to talk back more often; they don't listen as well as they used to; they seem abusive; they are disrespectful of authority. These new behavior patterns have bewildered many teachers and have driven some out of the profession. Assistant principals find themselves punishing and suspending the same students over and over again. Many students in the inner-city schools turn sullen and drop out psychologically as early as grade two. Suburban students are not far behind.

8

In working with numerous school staffs, I made one final observation related to loneliness in the schools. Lacking staff cohesiveness and adequate communication, most schools have no clearly defined philosophy or common direction. I asked many faculties, What is the philosophy of this school in relation to student discipline? They answer by producing bulletins and handbooks along with many unenforceable rules, and it soon becomes apparent that there are almost as many philosophies as there are teachers. Another question I asked is, What kind of learner is this school trying to develop? Answers usually indicate that although each teacher has his own ideas, rarely has there been enough discussion leading to any kind of working consensus.

More than 20 years ago, a White House Conference on Education was told by then President Killian of M. I. T. that:

> It is obviously vital for this Conference to open with an examination of goals. We cannot proceed in any orderly way to build, staff and finance a school until we agree on the job we want the school to do. Many misunderstandings can be cleared up when more immediate "practical" problems are considered. Too often school problems are discussed backwards — beginning with demanding day-to-day matters and working back slowly — and perhaps never getting to fundamental principles . . . People who disagree on the fundamental principles cannot easily agree on school budgets, or on much of anything else connected with education.

Dr. William Glasser, speaking before the National Association of Elementary School Principals, described his Schools Without Failure Program, which had completed three years of nationwide operation. In his speech Dr. Glasser stated:

> A school without failure first of all has to
> have a faculty without failure. You can't have
> a faculty feeling failure . . . A faculty that feels
> we don't care much about each other . . .
> A faculty that doesn't interact with each other
> and feel friendly and involved. And this is
> again something easy to say, but it has to
> be done. And it can only be done if you set
> a time to do it.

Glasser's words make a great deal of sense to me, since I have repeatedly observed a direct correlation between involved faculties and involved students. ***The staff must get involved in order to help the students get involved.***

Loneliness is a condition that nobody wants. Anyone may choose to be alone, but no one chooses to be lonely. Yet as I pointed out, under certain conditions schools can be very lonely places. When those conditions, which I refer to as separators or separation factors, exist the soil is ripe for loneliness. If even one person in a school feels this separation-induced loneliness, this mood communicates itself and may become contagious. Whether students feel alienated from their classmates or teacher or whether teachers feel that staff members and administrators don't care about them, they feel the same—lonely.

The next four chapters describe what keeps people in schools alienated from one another. Becoming aware of these separation factors may help us begin to make judgments and plans to avoid or overcome these tendencies in the future.

CHAPTER TWO

WHAT KEEPS STUDENTS

APART?

APART

APART

APART

Children are naturally gregarious. They are always looking for friends — in the park, on the streets, on the beach, in the school, everywhere. It is in the schools, however, where they come together in large groups for a common purpose and have to be "managed." Do we manage them in the best ways? What do we do in the schools that causes students to feel apart and turned off? Do any of the following practices sound familiar? Are they necessary? Can some be eliminated or modified without creating chaos or confusion?

STATIC ABILITY-GROUPING

For years educators have paid lip service to meeting individual student needs and differences. Courses in education and psychology have proclaimed a need for taking the student where he is and helping him move along according to his ability and desire. What really happens in most of our tradition-bound and overcrowded classrooms is that students are locked into groups based on some standardized achievement or IQ test, and there they stay immobilized in their proper place on the bell curve!

Most teachers who group students do not usually move them up as they achieve and progress. This happens in the traditional three reading groups, which still afflict most of our classrooms, and in partially departmentalized and ability-grouped programs. The consequences of this kind of inadequate ability grouping are:

■ An elite is created. All students know their place. No one is fooled. In some schools, a status-seeking competition develops, with knowledgeable parents constantly pressuring their children to move into the top group. In less academically oriented communities, low groupers realize that they are separated from the "smart" kids and experience feelings of discouragement and failure. The argument that "that's the way life is" isn't really sound, because in life if you are in a bad situation, you can usually get out. Students who are required by law to attend school have no such option.

■ Most students tend to perform according to the expectations of the group in which they are placed. This is fine if they are overplaced and encouraged to meet the expectations of that group, but this is usually not so. Research tells us that students, more often than not, perform according to teacher expectations. This is why they are seldom moved ahead or back once they are placed. Our criterion for placement leaves much to be desired. The theory that groups are flexible rarely is put into practice, and the students usually are "in for the duration."

■ When we group students in this way, we are keeping them apart by discouraging interaction among members of the class. Observation will show that the students in the low group often stick together both in and out of the classroom and tend to get into social difficulty more often than the top group. In other words, academic isolation often unintentionally creates social isolation.

Ability grouping is by no means all bad. Much educational research has indicated a need for some of it in order to adjust the learning environment to individual learning rates and styles. Dividing large classrooms into more manageable units is also necessary for teacher convenience and survival. Anyone who has to work with large groups of students for six hours a day knows this is true. Teaching twelve students of relatively similar ability is certainly more effective than working with thirty-six students of varying abilities. But when we are with the group of twelve, we should ask ourselves, What are those other twenty-four really

learning? Are there better alternatives to our traditional modes
of ability grouping?

AGE/GRADE PLACEMENT

When a new student enters a school, someone in the office will
look at his age, report card, and former placement. The student
will then be assigned to a classroom at the appropriate grade
level, where he will stay and presumably function at or close to
the norm for students his age. This is efficient and traditional, and
it will probably not adversely affect most students. However, this
procedure does isolate him from both older and younger students.
It precludes the possibilities of developing positive relationships
with older students or of developing responsibility for helping
and modeling appropriate behavior for younger students in a
classroom situation. Opportunities are also reduced for positive
interaction among multi-age groups on the playground. More
contact among these groups could help eliminate the conflicts
between the second and third grades, fifth and sixth grades, and
so on. Unfortunately, traditional placement practices often limit
opportunities to certain grade levels, such as participation in student
government and other special school activities.

ISOLATION OF SPECIAL OR HANDICAPPED STUDENTS

Educators make a practice of separating students who are
different from the accepted norm. If a student doesn't "fit-in" or
is handicapped, he is removed from contact with the rest of the
school population. This is done with the deaf, blind, crippled,
mentally retarded, socially maladjusted, emotionally disturbed,
and a large new category called the educationally handicapped.
These students are placed in special classes in order to help them
become more effective and more productive members of our
society. This is commendable, for special students need qualified

people to give them specialized help, but they should be returned *to the regular classroom to practice their newly learned skills.* Unfortunately, when we take them out of the regular classroom, we usually remove them from the real world, increasing their separateness and calling attention to their differences. Furthermore, we deprive students in the regular classrooms of the beneficial reciprocity of interacting with their handicapped peers. Are there ways in which we can give exceptional students the help they need without separating them from the mainstream of school life?

What's-the-use?

PHYSICAL ORGANIZATION OF THE
SCHOOL AND CLASSROOM

Because the school is an institution, efficiency often takes
precedence over humanness in the organization of the environment.
This causes problems in the schools because learning, which is
the reason for the schools' existence, requires intensive human
interaction. Most schools preclude such interaction by
compartmentalizing students and teachers and by creating such
barriers to human contact as fences, walls, locks, and grade-level
separation of classrooms.

Classrooms are often arranged in ways that separate students
from each other. Unitized desks and other difficult to handle
compartmentalized furniture often lock the classroom into a seating
pattern in which the back of someone's head is the most common
view. I still see many first-grade classrooms designed with single
desks, which keep all students three feet apart. Although static
furniture arrangements are easier to maintain, many schools have
abandoned them in favor of more friendly and involving room
environments.

CURRICULAR AND INSTRUCTIONAL SEPARATORS

It is beyond the scope of this book to delve deeply into teaching
theory and methods. However, a brief look at four factors in this
field may help in evaluating school practices in terms of student
separation.

Overuse of Work Sheets and Workbooks

Technology enables us to reproduce in the local school large
quantities of follow-up reading materials and work sheets in
other subject areas. These, coupled with commercial materials,

are available in great quantity and give teachers an almost inexhaustible reservoir of fill-in, check-off, and match-up work sheets with which to keep students busy and quiet in their seats. Some of this paper work, particularly that designed by teachers to meet a specific learning objective, is excellent. Some is very hard to read and of little educational value.

I observed in many schools that overuse of this material (referred to by some perceptive teachers as "the purple plague") has some undesirable side effects. First, it steals time from students who could be working together to set and reach new learning goals, working with the teacher, or exploring learning centers and the library. Second, work sheets are rarely used to give students immediate (within five minutes) feedback on skills that need to be improved. Third, as students begin to realize that the teacher often has an unlimited supply of busywork that they can never finish, they develop undesirable work habits and become easily distracted. In more affluent areas, students will put up with this paper work more readily than in many inner-city schools, where students' work is either ignored or destroyed.

Unfair Competitive Practices

Competition may be the lifeblood of our economy and fair competition is often a healthy incentive. But to place a student with learning problems in intellectual competition with a consistently high achiever in front of his peers is cruel. This unfair competition contributes to loneliness and separation in the classroom. In classrooms all over the country there are still practices going on that perpetuate unfair competition. The losers always know who they are, and their identification with failure is reinforced. Spelling bees, posted test scores, reading contests, unattainable reward offers, recitations, and

Students are locked into groups.

oral reading in front of the class tend to make some students feel as though school isn't a very good place for them.

Report Cards

Traditional A-B-C-D-F marking systems create a student caste system. When report cards are given out, students gather together at the end of the day and compare marks. How many **A's** did you get? Again, the failures feel alienated. For some, it is no contest. They never received an **A** and probably never will.

They have documented confirmation of their failure, and unless they receive a great deal of positive reinforcement at home or somewhere else to counteract this failure, they feel very lonely in a school environment that associates success with high marks.

Testing

In theory, educational testing has as its main purpose the **diagnosis** of student learning needs. In practice, however, most tests used in schools serve only to sort and classify students for the purpose of grading. Memorized information and the most easily measurable skills have been the basic assessment targets of the expedient and overused objective test. Teacher-made testing instruments generally are more useful and less harmful than the proliferous standardized testing programs being ushered in with the era of accountability.

The growing trend of using test scores to classify students and schools contributes to student separation and is a perversion of the original purpose of learning assessment.[2] When students are continuously measured against a norm based on questionable standards and are found wanting, they experience a feeling of failure and its attendant loneliness. Assessment for the purpose of diagnosing important learning needs is helpful only when the testing information is used to help students move successfully through school according to their individual learning rates and styles.

THE LUNCH PERIOD

Large numbers of students crowded together in relatively small eating areas often prompt educators to impose unreasonable

---

[2] The **Los Angeles Times** publishes the results of State Testing Programs by grade level and school, including average school IQ scores and percentages of minority students.

and unenforceable restrictions on student interaction during the lunch period. Frustrated teachers or noon directors desperately call for order and sometimes insist that students do not talk with each other either at the tables or in the serving lines. Much frustration and many power struggles result in this futile effort to prevent students from talking together while they eat. Some schools have developed creative approaches to solving this separation problem. What alternatives to the current system of organizing the lunch period have you seen or heard about? What changes could make lunchtime more pleasant and generally communal?

NO TALKING IN CLASS

There are times in life and in school when quiet is definitely needed by teachers and students alike. When I taught reading, I had a rather low noise tolerance level and couldn't work effectively with students if there was a lot of conversation going on. The class knew my limits and usually tried to keep the talking down. I don't believe this reasonable accommodation hurt the students. I have been in schools, however, where all two-way communication was stifled. There was no talking unless it was teacher initiated and directed. Many of us in the teaching profession still have this preoccupation with quiet. Our professional conditioning reassures us that if the students are busy and not talking, all is going well, even if it is not.

Research and common sense are disillusioning us about the quietness fetish. In fact, we are beginning to recognize it as a deterrent to learning and a definite factor in preventing students from interacting in educationally important ways.

DO YOUR OWN WORK

How many times do we hear and say, Keep your eyes on your

Teachers find themselves in separate classrooms doing their own thing.

own paper! I'll tear up your paper if I see you doing that again! Is this really your own work?

Is it wrong for students who know more or who have special skills to help students who are having difficulty? I don't think so. Not only will the less capable student be helped, but the more capable will improve. The eyes-on-your-own-paper philosophy is a product of our eternal preoccupation with accountability to the colleges; i.e., getting students ready for the tell-them-and-test-them system that is being more and more discredited as technology and learning theory become more sophisticated.

Keeping students from helping each other is a separator that often inhibits learning, encourages unfair competition, and lets students know we don't trust them. Many teachers find numerous creative ways to determine levels of learning and rates of progress without separating students from each other. What are some ways in which you could encourage students to help each other learn? Could you develop a peer-teaching program in cooperation with other teachers?

THE LINEUP

Tradition has us lining up students to go everywhere. While this technique is useful for crowd control, it removes personal responsibility for moving from place to place within the school in reasonable order. Lines may be necessary when people need to take their turn, but most lineups probably cause teachers more trouble than they are worth.

LACK OF EMPHASIS ON SOCIALIZATION SKILLS

Traditionally, schools were concerned only with the three R's. Later on they got involved with what was called social studies, which in abstract ways emphasized how people lived and got along with one another. Emphasis is now needed on the *specifics* of group process in the classroom, including how to make friends and how to develop both personal and group responsibility. Without direct and planned experiences in these areas, many students will continue to find themselves isolated and unable to function effectively in school and in life.

Many of our problems today are due to our lack of respect for each other as persons. It makes sense to begin learning in school, as early as possible, to respect each other and our social-cultural

"The Purple Plague."

differences. This kind of effort is built into too few school environments. Because of this lack of emphasis, we are perpetuating caste systems which segregate people who differ economically, ethnically, and racially. Although the schools cannot solve all social problems, they may be able to help in some important areas.

Planning Sheet 1

DIAGNOSIS

Do any of these factors in your school separate students from each other? Number in order of priority for action what you consider to be the most significant separation factors.

_____ Ability grouping

_____ Age/grade placement

_____ Isolation of special or handicapped students

_____ Physical organization of the school and classroom

_____ Curricular or instructional separators

    _____ Overuse of work sheets or workbooks

    _____ Unfair competitive practices

    _____ Report cards

    _____ Testing

_____ The lunch period

_____ No talking in class

_____ Do your own work

_____ The lineup

_____ Lack of emphasis on socialization skills

_____ Other separators that keep students uninvolved and lonely (add your own)

Planning Sheet 1

NOTES

Tradition has us lining up students to go everywhere.

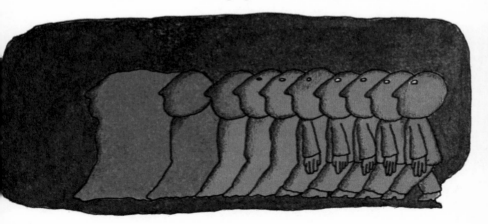

TAKING CORRECTIVE ACTION

Working Alone

Ask yourself the following questions:
Which separation factors in my school need immediate attention?
What can I do about them? Are any of these separators a matter
of school policy? If so, what can I do about changing the policy?

■ Read Chapter 6 for ideas about what to do.

■ Discuss these separators with the students in your classroom.

■ Try to involve at least one colleague in a discussion of these
ideas and the above questions. Can you work together to
eliminate any of the separators?

Working in a Group

After reading Chapter 6, try the following process for deciding on
priorities for action. This is an effective method for developing
a consensus. It's not easy, but it works.

■ Each person in the group decides individually on the ranking
of these or other separators.

■ Form smaller groups of four to six people. Compare your
individual rankings and try to agree on priorities. *Keep the
discussion focused on what you can agree on, even if it
is only on one point. Do not vote on or average out your
decisions.* Continue the discussion until you reach partial
agreement on some priorities for action.

■ With the entire group, discuss again, as outlined above,
until agreement is reached on at least one separator that the
group will attempt to eliminate.

Planning Sheet 1

NOTES

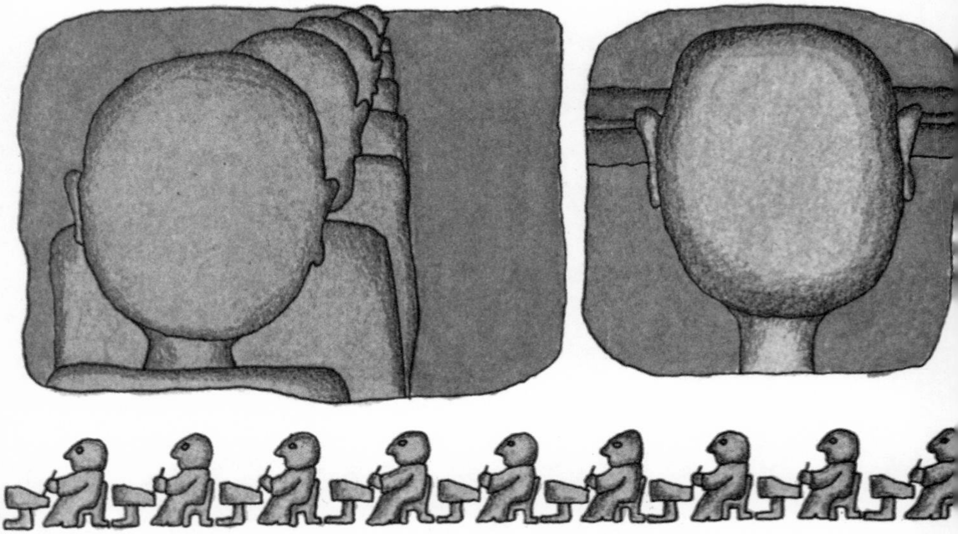

The back of someone's head is the most common view.

CHAPTER THREE

WHAT KEEPS STUDENTS AND TEACHERS

APART?

APART

APART

APART

Students are coming to school with significantly different attitudes than they had ten years ago. As early as kindergarten, they are asking existential questions. "Am I a good person?" "Who likes me at school?" "Where do I fit in here?" They are demanding increased personal involvement in order to establish themselves in relation to other students and teachers *within a system that traditionally placed a low priority on this kind of interaction.* Although intuition and common sense tell teachers that they should become involved with students before they can teach them subject matter or skills, human involvement activities rarely are included in their lesson plans. The system, with its emphasis on testing and memorizing, automatically builds in certain policies, programs, and practices that result in many lonely, unmotivated students and frustrated teachers.

Let's examine some of the factors that continue to keep students separated from the most important adult in the school—the teacher. Remember that these separators are vestiges of another era and can be changed by concerted staff effort. How can you eliminate these traditional separators from your school?

LACK OF PLANNED SUCCESS PRACTICES

In spite of all that is known about the powerful effect of success as a motivator, many teachers are unable to use this knowledge in motivating students, since they work within a system that focuses on failure. Testing is used to sort and classify students, with the main emphasis placed on finding failures, who would then be given remedial work. Misdirected discipline isolates the students who are not making it—either by excluding them from the mainstream of school, or by grouping them together in social adjustment, or euphemistically called opportunity rooms.

Fortunately, many teachers, working around the system, are developing great skill in identifying and reinforcing successful student behavior through activities that I refer to as success practices.

Success practices are planned activities initiated by the teacher and directed toward building self-worth in students. These activities usually reduce classroom tensions, promote positive personal involvement between teacher and student, and make teaching more enjoyable. Teachers throughout the country are developing and implementing hundreds of success practices and gradually are turning the system away from its present focus on failure toward more professionally rewarding directions. Examples of success practices may be found in Chapter 6.

LACK OF JOINT SUCCESS ENDEAVORS

When students and teachers participate together in an enjoyable activity, they feel pleased. Unfortunately, opportunities for such joint endeavors are limited in most school situations.

Too often teachers are so pressured into raising reading test scores, covering the new state-mandated curriculum, or experimenting with some new method of teaching that there is little or no opportunity for students and teachers to plan and participate in mutually rewarding success experiences. If such experiences could be built into the curriculum, separation between teachers and their students would be markedly reduced. Activities such as plays, song fests, film seminars, class car washes, ball games, picnics, and field trips help build teacher-student involvement. Can you think of other joint success activities?

INCRIMINATING SCHOOL RECORDS

School records, including IQ and achievement test scores and subjective teacher observations, can often determine teacher

There are many unmotivated students and frustrated teachers.

attitudes toward a student. This information will often unduly influence teacher expectations and may occasionally cause difficulty when classes are being arranged for a new school year. Dividing up the "difficult" or "problem" students on the basis of their records is an annual game played in every school—the rules varying according to the relationship between teachers and administrators. Unfortunately, no matter how it works out, the teacher who receives the file of a problem student expects certain behavior patterns, prepares for that behavior, and is usually not disappointed. In addition to formal records, informal teacher conversations regarding students with problems often cruelly brand those students and reduce their chances for a fresh start. In any case, teacher and student often are separated psychologically simply on the basis of what social psychologists call the "self-fulfilling prophecy."

Students who are not succeeding in school have a lonely road to travel. Negative comments by teachers or principals regarding so-called problem students generally do little to clear their path and usually aggravate already painful situations. Ways must be found to prevent this from happening. The question needs to be asked: What is the role of the teacher and administrator in maintaining confidential relationships with students?

PHYSICAL ROOM ARRANGEMENT

Traditionally, most intermediate, upper-grade, and some primary teachers are at the front of the classroom, dispensing information for a great part of the school day. This procedure is slowly changing as teachers are moving their desks aside. However, I observed that the traditional room arrangement still predominates. Students face the teacher and the back of each other's heads. It is only natural that both teacher and student feel separated under this physical arrangement. With the teacher at the head of the line or in front of the class for most of the day, chances are slim that student and teacher can interact on a warm, friendly, and personal level. What are the alternatives to this traditional classroom arrangement? What are the advantages of having more involving room arrangements?

RIGHT-ANSWER PEDAGOGY

Teacher insistence on one right answer and a single process for solving problems stifles creativity, chloroforms thinking, and may cause a personal separation between teacher and student. If the student feels that he must know a certain answer in order to survive, he may learn it. However, this method will not necessarily make him feel close to the teacher or free to explore alternative methods of seeking solutions to problems. The student who cannot memorize or understand the one-answer process may give up and withdraw from the entire school operation as well as from the teacher as a person.

John Holt eloquently describes the strategies that students develop in desperate attempts to achieve human involvement as they try to save face in front of the teacher and their peers when they don't know the right answer.[3] Through the use of traditional questioning methods, students are often unintentionally humiliated before their peers. This is another factor that moves teachers and students further apart.

NOT KNOWING ENOUGH ABOUT THE STUDENT'S WORLD

Students are now coming to school loaded with information. James Coleman's article "The Children Have Outgrown the Schools" deals with this phenomenon at some length.[4] More learning opportunities are now available for students outside of school rather than inside, which is a reversal of the traditional roles. Educators are desperately trying to find ways in which the schools can more adequately meet the needs of today's student. Failure to be adequately informed about students' interests and activities outside of school not only reduces a teacher's effectiveness, but also precludes many opportunities for forming closer bonds with students, since genuine communication is rooted in a shared interest.

What do you believe to be the most practical way of learning about the needs and interests of the students in your classroom and school?

---

[3] John Holt, *How Children Fail* (New York: Pitman Publishing Co., 1964).

[4] James Coleman, "The Children Have Outgrown the Schools," *Psychology Today,* February 1972, pp. 72-75.

UNENFORCEABLE RULES

In almost every school that I visit, there are rules, such as "no running in the halls or corridors," which are not enforceable to any effective degree. When such rules are imposed without student involvement and discussion, situations develop which further separate students from teachers. The teachers feel obligated to enforce the rule, but since the rule is meaningless to the student, it continually is violated. We then have a no-win situation in which teacher and student are alienated from one another. Alternative ways of improving discipline through reasonable rules, natural consequences, and positive teacher-student involvement are being demonstrated with success in many schools across the country.

FEAR OF PUNISHMENT

A problem related to that of unenforceable rules is the fear of punishment, which prevents many students from developing comfortable and mutually rewarding relationships with their teachers. Punishment can be defined as the infliction of pain on someone in the hope that he will not repeat a given action. The pain of punishment is not always physical. Sarcasm, ridicule, and humiliation often hurt students more than the belt or the paddle. It is known that the infliction of emotional pain is not an effective punishment. In schools where this form of punishment is used, the separation between teachers and students increases. What types of punishment are most frequently used or resorted to in your school? What practical alternatives to punishment could you develop in your school?

Testing is used to sort and classify students.

Planning Sheet 2
DIAGNOSIS

Do any of these factors in your school separate students and teachers? Number in order of priority for action what you consider to be the most significant separators.

_____ Lack of planned success practices

_____ Lack of joint success endeavors

_____ Incriminating school records

_____ Physical room arrangements

_____ Right-answer pedagogy

_____ Not knowing enough about the student's world

_____ Unenforceable rules

_____ Fear of punishment

_____ Other separators that keep students and teachers from relating in positive and friendly ways (add your own)

Planning Sheet 2

NOTES

Insistence on one right answer stifles creativity.

TAKING CORRECTIVE ACTION

Working Alone

Ask yourself some questions related to the topic in this chapter such as: Am I satisfied with the physical arrangement of my classroom? If not, how could it be changed so that I become more positively involved with my class? Do I know enough about what my students do when they are not in school? How could I talk to them about some of their off-campus activities? When was the last time the class and I did something together that was fun for all of us? Could we plan another such activity? Then:

- Read Chapter 6 for ideas.

- Discuss some of the ideas in this chapter with your class or other students in the school.

- Find a colleague with whom to discuss success strategies and select those that you could work on together.

Working in a Group

Follow the directions for the group-consensus activity in Planning Sheet 1 (page 28). Then hold a staff meeting for the sole purpose of brainstorming ways to become more positively involved with the students in your school.[5]

---

[5] For useful information on the technique of brainstorming, I recommend: Charles Clark, *Brainstorming* (Garden City, New York: Doubleday & Co., 1958).

Planning Sheet 2

NOTES

Fear of punishment prevents students from developing rewarding relationships with teachers.

CHAPTER FOUR

WHAT SEPARATES TEACHERS FROM EACH

OTHER?

OTHER

OTHER

OTHER

The backbone of a successful school is a staff composed of persons who are positively involved with each other, who **care** about each other, who work cooperatively, and who plan together in the best interests of the students.

Professional satisfaction, success, and feelings of personal worth seem to increase in direct proportion to the closeness among staff members. In schools where I worked and visited, closeness among teachers accompanied a corresponding closeness among students. As a school staff works closely and effectively together, a better educational environment, smoother working conditions, and greater professional satisfaction results. Why then are so many school staffs alienated and fragmented? What keeps the members apart? After asking hundreds of teachers these questions, I identified the following separation factors.

SIZE OF SCHOOL

Parents and professional educators alike would probably agree that a smaller school has a better chance to develop a pleasant and effective learning environment than a larger one. In a small school, everyone knows each other. The principal is usually accessible. Students recognize and interact more with teachers.

An elementary school of 1,600 to 2,000 enrollment is almost impossible to manage effectively without a large staff and a built-in flexibility in the assignment of time and special services. I recall visiting a colleague recently assigned as principal of a large inner-city school. After two months on the job, he still did not know the names of the personnel in the building. His span of control was so tenuous that any business management consultant would have written the situation off as unworkable. Few teachers who find themselves in large school situations such as this know or care about each other. They may make a few friends, but as far as professional involvement is concerned, there is little hope for sustained and productive personal contact.

In junior and senior high schools, which are usually larger than elementary schools, alienation and estrangement among staff members is even more pronounced.

CLIQUES, GRADE LEVELS AND DEPARTMENTS

Closely related to the size of schools as a separation factor among the adults who work there is its structural organization. The tendency for teachers to stick close together based on their mutual interests often divides them into grade-level and department cliques. Kindergarten and primary teachers are usually isolated physically, often having their own playground areas and schedules. Upper-grade teachers tend to stick together as do the department members in the high schools. Some of these separations naturally are built into the school structure and cannot be avoided. Too often, however, they are divisive factors which prevent a continuity of communication through the various levels; this results in a broad variation in teacher standards, which confuses students and creates a barrier to the development of effective school policies.

THAT TRAPPED FEELING

A friend, who is the principal of a school in Florida, told me that one of the finest teachers in his school recently came into his office and said desperately, "Charlie, hope you don't mind, but I just have to talk to someone over ten years old!"

When a teacher leaves the classroom to become an administrator, consultant, supervisor, or director, it is easy for him to forget very quickly what it was like to be a teacher. Being assigned to and responsible for a class of thirty or more students for six hours a day, five days a week, is not an easy job. Administrators need to remember that as teachers they often dragged themselves to work— even though they were ill—in order not to let the kids down; they answered the bells and rushed to the classroom; they were trapped on rainy days when they really needed to get away from the sights, sounds, and smells of the classroom, if only for ten minutes.

A local school administrator who stops thinking like a teacher and stops empathizing with teacher frustrations and concerns sacrifices a great part of his potential effectiveness and credibility in relating to a school staff. Recognition and discussion of teacher isolation is essential in relieving that trapped feeling and broadening the scope of professional interaction of all staff members.

THE SELF-CONTAINED CLASSROOM

Traditionally, the institution of one teacher to one class is the basic instructional unit of the elementary school. Fortunately, many alternatives to the self-contained classroom—schools without walls, teaming, departmentalization, and open structure—have developed within the last few years. Change comes slowly, however, and most school districts have self-contained classrooms and will continue to have them for a long time. There are some distinct advantages to the single-unit classroom, but it does tend to separate teachers from one another. How often have you seen teachers bristle when one of their colleagues corrected "their class"? How often have teachers held on to more than their share of supplies or textbooks so that "their class" wouldn't be deprived?

Interaction among teachers is limited by the self-contained classroom, but in many traditionally organized schools creative approaches to more cooperative teaching are being developed successfully.

Recognition and discussion of teacher isolation is essential in relieving that trapped feeling.

STAFF MEETINGS

Ask any teacher—most faculty meetings are crashing bores. Not only are they boring, but they usually are unproductive, things going along pretty much the same after the meetings as before. That's not much of a testimonial to their effectiveness.

One of the reasons why faculty meetings fail so frequently is that most teachers are worn out at the end of the school day. Furthermore, most meetings are exercises in one-way communication that neither inform nor inspire. I endured many meetings during which teachers sat together in the same room but were mutually tuned out and psychologically separated from each other. This is not what boards of education had in mind when they mandated staff meetings as a part of the total school operation.

Many local school administrators, becoming increasingly disenchanted with weekly faculty meetings, abandon all attempts at getting the staff together. As I see it, the trend is toward fewer meetings instead of improved and useful meetings—a trend that will surely *increase* separation among the members of a school staff.

NOT KNOWING EACH OTHER

I recently worked with a large faculty in an attempt to help them communicate more effectively and develop a consensus on their school philosophy. As teachers began to talk together on a more personal level, several of them discovered that they shared the same hobbies, interests, and surprisingly enough, even had mutual friends. These teachers were working together in the same school, and some in the same department, for five to fifteen years as virtual strangers.

Teachers need to know each other as persons in order to work together effectively and professionally. This doesn't mean that they must be close friends or plan their social lives around the school.

But there seems to be a direct correlation between the friendliness among teachers and the climate of learning for the students. In schools where teachers truly are well acquainted, compared with those in which this is not true, there seems to be: 1) more consideration in planning and sharing the use of time and supplies, 2) less defensiveness, 3) more consensus and sense of direction, and 4) a more hospitable climate for the assimilation of new personnel.

LACK OF CONSENSUS

In a school where people work closely together as associates and colleagues, it is important that they be able to reach agreement on what they are trying to do together and how they plan to do it. In fact, this should be the prime consideration in a school. Working together to reach agreements should be the cement that binds people to one another to make a good school instead of a collection of isolated individuals in insulated classrooms. Unfortunately, this is not the case. In most schools not enough time is set aside for staff members to discuss and come to a common agreement on important issues or to resolve differences in standards and values. As the hour grows late and teachers become tired, the usual procedure for settling a problem is to vote. Often the result of the vote is close to 60% for and 40% against, leaving nearly half of the staff unhappy with the decision and uninterested in initiating it. This voting process, so commonly adopted in an election, can be a destructive and alienating factor when applied to the resolution of school issues.

FEAR OF INADEQUACY

Many teachers are separated from each other by fears and anxieties that develop due to the structure and organization of the school. As already mentioned, the self-contained classroom sometimes causes teachers to feel that their class is their only responsibility and that they have little else to do with the overall school operation.

But there are other less tangible factors that tend to cause fear and anxiety in teachers by placing them in unspoken competition with each other. Not measuring up on local, state, or national tests, not being "in" with the administrator or favored teacher group, not being selected as a training teacher, not being asked to demonstrate a new activity or program are considered to be real inadequacies by certain staff members. As a result, meetings often become contests with teachers vying for approval and recognition.

Incidents that place teachers in personal and professional conflict with each other occur daily in almost any school. As schools become even more open to the public and as outside demands become more intense, these staff-relation problems will increase. These conditions will require a greater climate of trust among staff members, and their cooperation with one another will become a matter of professional survival. *Without this trusting climate, fear, suspicion, envy, and apathy will increase in direct proportion to outside pressures.*

ISOLATION OF SPECIAL EDUCATION TEACHERS

Many teachers of intellectually, emotionally, or physically handicapped students within the regular school find themselves in a constant struggle to avoid professional second-class citizenship. I talked with teachers of the blind, deaf, mentally retarded, and educationally handicapped, who feel that they literally are not a part of the school staff. Their schedules are different, their classes are separated from those of other students, and their routine prevents social and professional contact with other staff members.

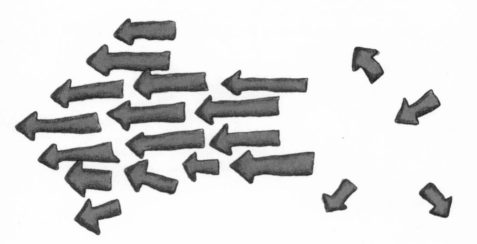

Working together to reach consensus binds people to one another.

As a result of such separations, which still are all too common in both elementary and secondary schools, valuable professional contributions are lost from teachers who are often superbly trained and who have much to offer in helping a school develop and improve.

COMPETING PROFESSIONAL ORGANIZATIONS

Teachers have come a long way professionally since the days when they were totally taken for granted and summarily dismissed without cause. Teachers' organizations are playing a decisive part in improving teacher status and education in general. But in spite of their positive accomplishments, they also cause separations.

Several questions may serve to point out the problem. What happens to a staff when some teachers join or actively participate in teachers' organizations, and some do not? What happens when there are two or more teachers' organizations actively competing for membership within the same school? What happens when active and philosophical splits develop among staff members regarding the function of professional organizations? What happens when a teachers' strike divides a faculty, with some staff members staying on the job and others walking the picket line?

LACK OF TIME FOR STAFFS TO GET TOGETHER

It takes time for teachers to get to know each other, for a school to develop a working philosophy based on consensus, and for teachers to reach agreement on important school problems. Yet time for people to get together is in short supply in all schools. Teachers and administrators always seem to be struggling to find adequate time to meet in order to deal with important issues, but they usually end up rushing through and leaving everyone frustrated, confused, and often alienated. Creative and cooperative planning of the use of time for staff and total school development would do much to reduce the growing estrangement among school faculties.

Planning Sheet 3

DIAGNOSIS

Do any of these factors in your school separate teachers from one another? Number in order of priority for action what you consider to be the most significant separation factors.

_____ Size of school

_____ Cliques, grade levels, and departments

_____ That trapped feeling

_____ The self-contained classroom

_____ Staff meetings

_____ Not knowing each other

_____ Lack of consensus

_____ Fear of inadequacy

_____ Isolation of special education leaders

_____ Competing professional organizations

_____ Lack of time to get together

_____ Other separators that keep teachers apart (add your own)

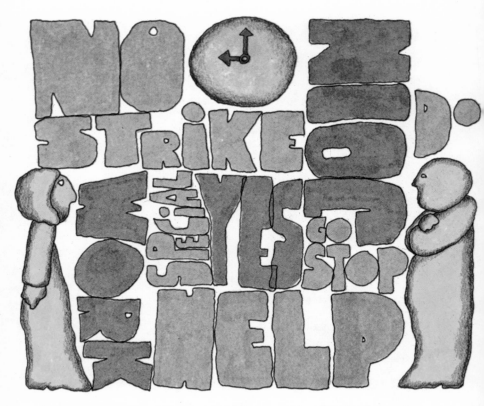

Many teachers are separated from each other by fears that develop due to the structure.

Planning Sheet 3

NOTES

TAKING CORRECTIVE ACTION

Working Alone

Ask yourself some very private questions about your relationship with other staff members. Questions such as: Am I a member of a clique? If so, is it damaging my relationships with those outside the clique? Do I sometimes feel trapped in the classroom or school? Have I ever relieved a colleague who felt trapped? When was the last time I complained about staff meetings? What have I done to improve them? Can I do anything to improve them? Have I ever reached out to a teacher who didn't seem happy at school?

- Read Chapter 7 for ideas.

- Discuss the ideas in this chapter with your friends and colleagues.

- Make a plan to become better acquainted with one adult in in the school.

Working in a Group

Follow the directions for the group-consensus activity in Diagnostic Check List 1 (page 28). Then plan some specific ways to correct your high priority separators with the staff. Consider the following brief planning guidelines:

- Does everyone understand the problem?

- What is going to be done about it? State specific expectations and goals.

- Who is going to do what? What will be the specific tasks and commitments of the people carrying out the plan?

- What is the allotted time for the plan? **Write down** dates by which certain expectations are to be realized and evaluate progress at those times.

Planning Sheet 3

NOTES

Planning Sheet 3

NOTES

CHAPTER FIVE

ADMINISTRATIVE FACTORS IN

STAFF

SEPARATION

STAFF

STAFF

STAFF

I recently saw a sign on an elementary principal's desk that expressed a growing sentiment: "Looking for someone with a little authority? I have as little as anyone." This facetious statement reflects what many local school administrators feel is happening to them. I discussed this problem with administrators in all parts of the country. On the one hand, I find the consensus to be that the responsibility of the principal is increasing in terms of accountability requirements, community demands, and special programs and budgets. On the other hand, his authority is diminishing because of teacher organization activities, increased community involvement, and changing relationships with upper-echelon administrators and boards of education. Principals are taking more sick leave and are retiring earlier as the pressures mount. Yet in spite of these changes the principal still remains the person who has the most influence on the personality of the school.[6]

Millions of words have been written about the role of the principal and the expectations that teachers and others have of him. There is no shortage of advice that suggests ways in which a local school administrator can improve his performance. Some of this advice is useful, and some is unrealistic. Unfortunately, very little of the advice is heeded, no matter how well-intentioned. Why? Because today most principals find themselves up to their armpits in alligators and unable to concentrate on their original objective, which is to drain the swamp. The alligators represent the multitude of emergency human-relations problems, which must be sorted out and handled in the schools each day. The swamp is the morass of factors that block the way to building a proper learning environment for students. The most outstanding factor is the growing alienation

---

[6] I define the personality of the school to be the quality of the environment of the school as determined by the interaction of the people who work and learn there.

Most principals find themselves up to their armpits in alligators.

among staff members who find themselves increasingly separated from each other and who are experiencing little professional satisfaction.

Because they are human, principals will sometimes act in ways which increase the separation among faculty members and widen the gap between principal and teachers. Principals must recognize these actions if the swamp is to be drained. Teachers must be aware of the relentless pressures that prevent local school administrators from performing in more effective and positive ways.

In my experience, teachers often mention the following administrator-related factors as inhibiting positive staff involvement.

LACK OF ACCESSIBILITY

This condition is described by teachers in many ways. The principal is never around. He is always going to meetings. His door is always closed. He won't talk to me without an appointment. He never eats lunch with us or comes into the faculty lounge. He is never in my room except to take notes for a performance report. He's not around when we need him to help with a staff or grade-level decision. He makes his decisions by the book, but he is never around to discuss the book with us.

The principal's time is spread far too thin in most schools. Better arrangements need to be made, for staff cohesiveness will not improve until the on-site visibility of the local school administrator begins increasing instead of decreasing.

PLAYING FAVORITES

Teachers often complain about the existence of in-groups and out-groups within faculties. These divisions are based upon whether or not certain teachers agree or disagree with the principal.

Some faculty members feel penalized because they do not always go along with an administrator's pet project or because they do not try to ingratiate themselves with the administration. The feeling exists in many schools that special privileges, the best classes, and coveted professional opportunities are given to the "favored few." Regardless of the reasons for the existence of such feelings, the results are the same—divided faculties and diminished professional effectiveness.

LACK OF STAFF INVOLVEMENT IN RELEVANT DECISION MAKING

According to Robert Owen,[7] trying to involve school staff members in decisions which do not concern them is as destructive as not involving the staff in decisions in which they have strong interest. Teachers often feel that they are asked to settle questions of little consequence or relevance while the really significant decisions are made by administrators and are handed down from the top.

IMPROPER DELEGATION OF RESPONSIBILITY

When a principal asks a willing but overworked teacher to do a job that the teacher obviously doesn't have time to do, frustration and resentment often result. The same happens when duties and responsibilities are assigned to staff members who have neither the authority nor the ability to carry them out or when unwilling staff members are subtly manipulated into assuming unwanted responsibilites. The usual outcome of these misguided delegations is an increase in human conflict within the school. Staff members feel disappointed or angry. Some strike out and some withdraw, but ultimately, the students suffer.

---

[7] Robert Owen, *Organizational Behavior In Schools* (Englewood Cliffs, New Jersey: Prentice Hall, 1970).

As face-to-face communication increases, trust will develop and separation will diminish.

INADEQUATE PERSONAL COMMUNICATION BETWEEN PRINCIPAL AND STAFF

As mentioned earlier, staff meetings in many schools have been abandoned or are continuing in ineffectual ways. But these alternatives, along with bulletins, notes, and the overused intercom, are not very helpful in bringing principals and teachers closer together. Lack of personal contact between principals and teachers often prevents administrators from correctly judging the intensity of faculty opinions and feelings regarding important school problems. As face-to-face communication increases, a climate of trust will slowly develop, and separation will diminish.

Replies from many principals concerning what keeps them from becoming closer to their faculties and what factors seem most to interfere with their efforts in building trust among staff members include the following.

LARGE SCHOOL STAFFS

The amount of personal contact between a principal and the faculty depends upon the size of that faculty and the energy and ingenuity of the principal. In a school with a faculty of over thirty-five people, teacher involvement with even the most energetic and ingenious administrator will be minimal.

INADEQUATE LOCAL ADMINISTRATOR CONTROL OVER SCHOOL STAFFING

The finest teachers are needed in schools that have the greatest problems. Unfortunately, personnel practices in most school districts do not meet this need. When principals are unable to obtain experienced or qualified teachers in "difficult" schools,

72

problems usually become so grave that all fine intentions are abandoned as the school staff merely attempts to survive.

In addition to this problem, many school districts are doing very little to assist principals in properly matching teachers to the philosophy and needs of a given school. For example, rigid punishment-oriented teachers are sometimes assigned or transferred to schools where such an attitude would be inimical to the total school program. Conversely, teachers trained in open education may be assigned arbitrarily to traditional schools, where they would lose their effectiveness.

INCREASING DISTRICT DEMANDS ON PRINCIPALS' TIME

It seems that whenever pressures increase on school boards and upper-echelon school administrators, it is relieved by transferring the problem to the local school principal. Example: Reading scores are low. Newspapers publish the scores and panic results. Each principal in the district is then asked to drop everything and submit a plan for raising scores in his school. Meetings take place on a crisis basis. Reports are required; deadlines are set; and memos rain down like confetti on the beleagured school. The same process begins again when mounting pressures are related to discipline, integration, sex education, or any other socially volatile issue. This process is becoming a way of life in many school districts and is drawing principals away from their primary leadership responsibilities.

INCREASING COMMUNITY PRESSURE

Communities are demanding greater participation in the local school. As PTA activity continues, as community advisory councils become a part of the school, and as local community demands for involvement increase, the principals' work load will grow. Since the principal has traditionally acted as the community-school liaison, it is difficult for him to delegate this job to others. He must therefore face additional responsibilities, which will further separate him from people in the school.

PROLIFERATING SPECIAL PROGRAMS

The responsibility for ESEA Title programs, feeding programs, head start, childrens' centers, state programs, plus a myriad of others in the school end up in the principal's lap. These special programs, along with community and local district demands, decrease the involvement of the principal with the staff and student body.

TEACHER ORGANIZATIONS

As militant activity by teachers' organizations increase, principals in many schools feel isolated from their staffs. Many local administrators find themselves facing grievance procedures more often, and they have fewer opportunities to mediate conflicts on a personal level. More and more principals are telling me that teachers' organizations are adopting the labor-management system as their model. In their role as managers, principals find it increasingly difficult to become positively involved with faculties.

The administrator-related separation factors mentioned above are disquieting, but they are not going to disappear. We must do our best to deal responsibly with the ones we have some control over, or we will continue to witness increasing separation among teachers and administrators at the expense of the teaching-learning environment of the school.

As managers, principals find it difficult to become positively involved with faculties.

Planning Sheet 4

DIAGNOSIS

Do any of these factors *separate the principal from the staff in your school?* Number in order of priority for action what you consider to be the most significant separation factors.

_____ Lack of accessibility

_____ Playing favorites

_____ Lack of staff involvement in relevant decision making

_____ Improper delegation of responsibility

_____ Inadequate personal communication between principal and staff

_____ Large school staff

_____ Inadequate local administrator control over school staffing

_____ Increasing district demands on principals' time

_____ Increasing community pressure

_____ Proliferating special programs

_____ Teacher organizations

_____ Other separators keeping principal and staff apart (add your own)

Planning Sheet 4

NOTES

Planning Sheet 4

TAKING CORRECTIVE ACTION

Now that you have identified and ranked these separators, read Chapter 7 and answer these questions. Answer them individually, then discuss them in a group *that includes the principal.*

■ What can the staff do to help reduce the pressures that separate the principal from his primary responsibilities to the people in the school?

■ What can the principal do to become more positively involved with the school staff?

In many schools special privileges are given to the "favored few."

Planning Sheet 4

NOTES

PART II

CHAPTER SIX

GETTING STUDENTS AND TEACHERS

The first step in getting students and teachers together is to determine what is keeping them apart. A review of the separation factors described in the previous sections should provide you with a frame of reference for this purpose. Teachers or principals who find none of these factors in their schools have no need for this book. However, if there are lonely and unsuccessful students and teachers in the school or classroom, some insight into their problems is necessary if the school is to become a better place in which to work and learn.

The next step is for your staff to begin talking together about those conditions which separate the people in your school.

Hopefully, these discussions will lead to plans for change. The staff needs to agree on priorities, and they must commit themselves to realizing their goals.

This chapter suggests ways in which people who work in schools can change the environment for the purpose of reducing loneliness and promoting success. The ideas and questions included are points of departure. They should be discussed, applied, modified, expanded, or rejected as staff members develop plans that best meet their local school needs.

USING SCHOOL LIVING SPACE
TO REDUCE LONELINESS

Today's television-oriented students do not stay involved with traditional teacher-up-front lessons. The less academically oriented tend to slip off into daydreams after about the first five minutes of class, and their classmates rapidly follow them. Class involvement deteriorates, the teacher struggles for attention, and discipline problems develop. By contrast, I observe many teachers who maintain high student interest in learning. They are the teachers who are often difficult to locate upon entering the classroom since they are almost never up front. Often they are working with a small group of students or are intensely involved with an individual pupil at his desk. A comfortable well-planned classroom arrangement seems basic to the development of an involving classroom atmosphere.

In attempting to find out how most creative and successful teachers plan their classroom arrangement and how they manage their class, the following common practices have been observed.

■ Involvement of students in planning and maintaining the classroom arrangement. Teachers have indicated that having students plan the classroom furniture arrangement is a powerful involvement factor. When students are asked to move furniture for a special lesson or discussion, they seem to become more interested in the activity and in each other. With teacher guidance, students at almost any grade level can plan and maintain class interest centers and bulletin boards. A number of discussions on planning classroom responsibilities should be held at the beginning of each year. This will improve the learning environment, and it will decrease discipline problems.

■ Involvement of students in changing the classroom environment as the learning situation warrants.

■ Allowance of students to select their own seats in class, as long as they act responsibly. This procedure seems to build a trusting relationship between teacher and class.

■ The use of classroom interest centers based on science, art, music, reading, mathematics, or special activities in which students can work and learn together. Flexible and rational rules that are carefully developed by both teacher and students are basic to the successful use of these centers.

86

■ Consideration of every available square foot of legally useable space, in and around the classroom, for learning activities. In many classrooms, tutoring centers are set up in little-used corridors and coatrooms.

■ Collection of comfortable old furniture—rocking chairs, carpeting, screens, old bus or airplane seats, and other items that will give the classroom a less institutional appearance. Students can make pillows and mats, and parents are often happy to contribute hand-me-downs to improve their child's classroom.

■ Placement of the teacher's desk in some out-of-the-way corner —a nook where teachers and students can confer privately.

■ Opening of the classroom doors on time and usually ahead of the bell—especially during inclement weather.

■ Maintenance of good relations with the school custodian, since the students in the class are involved in keeping their classroom clean and orderly. More and more students will volunteer for classroom housekeeping as they become involved with their peers and their teacher.

Many school cafeterias, auditoriums, and lunch rooms stand idle a large part of the day. Corridor and hall space is wasted. Libraries are either nonexistent or scheduled so tightly that no one uses them.

A school district in Utah expanded its ground floor classroom space by one-fourth—by moving into the corridors and cutting doors through to the classrooms from the outside. In San Diego, California, some infrequently used lunch rooms were converted by volunteers into starter libraries. Other schools use cafeterias and lunch areas as tutoring and learning centers. In increasing numbers creative teachers and administrators are exploring new ways of using space in the schools and classrooms.

WHAT ARE YOUR *IDEAS* FOR BETTER UTILIZATION OF THE LIVING SPACE IN YOUR SCHOOL OR CLASSROOM TO HELP BRING TEACHERS AND STUDENTS CLOSER TOGETHER?

HOW COULD YOU INVOLVE SOME OF THE SCHOOL STAFF IN DISCUSSIONS THAT WOULD USE THIS INFORMATION IN THINKING THROUGH SOME NECESSARY CHANGES IN YOUR OWN SCHOOL?

GROUPING STUDENTS TO REDUCE LONELINESS

Judicious use of school records is essential to proper grouping of students and contributes toward their success in school. Too often students are assigned haphazardly to classrooms merely on the basis of a test score, reading level, or a special teacher notation made in the student's records. In very large schools, this is often the most expedient method of setting up classes on those hectic first days of the school year. Unfortunately, the student makeup of these classes often stays the same or is reorganized later, but on a similar crisislike timetable.

If we are to increase the positive involvement of teacher and students, I would propose the following guidelines for organizing classes and grouping pupils.

■ That teachers **always** be involved in student placement—both the sending and receiving teachers and as many others as possible who are acquainted with the student being assigned.

■ That preplacement dialogue consider the **student as a person, not as a producer.** This will help avoid the reorganization "game of hearts" in which teachers discard slow and unmotivated students and try to assemble for themselves a class containing as many high achievers and as few discipline problems as possible. When students with learning, emotional, or social difficulties are all placed with the strongest teachers or all are passed off to new or inexperienced teachers, both types of teachers are being treated unfairly. In either case, teacher-student involvement, staff morale, and the general success of the school are jeopardized.

■ That grade-level grouping be flexible enough so that, if necessary, students can be exchanged and reassigned to a learning environment that is more beneficial to them. No placement need be considered as absolutely final. The introduction of multi-age grouping will provide for even greater flexibility in placement.

■ That placement of a student be considered in the positive light of the peers with whom he works best instead of those from whom he should be separated.

■ That, following student placement, teachers avoid as long as possible the use of school records for evaluation purposes. Teachers should find out for themselves who the students are and what they can do. Take a week to get acquainted—textbooks can wait. Discuss with students their expectations of school and tell them yours.

Integrating students with special learning problems and handicaps into the normal life of the school is becoming a national trend. Recent evidence indicates that the mainstreaming of most handicapped students is beneficial to the academic and social growth of both special and regular students. Programs for bringing handicapped students into the normal classroom are being successfully developed in many schools.

A school in San Diego, California, combined a class of eight deaf students with a regular class of thirty-five. Both the special teacher and the regular teacher were enthusiastic about the arrangement. When I observed the class, it was extremely difficult to locate the handicapped students. Except for an occasional lesson in lip reading or sign language, the deaf students were totally integrated and were participating in all class activities. A climate of mutual respect and trust among the students was clearly developing. The teachers stated that the deaf students were gaining self-confidence and, in several cases, were outperforming the regular sixth graders.

At some schools in California and Florida, another loneliness reducing method is used in teaching intellectually and emotionally handicapped students. Special resource teachers in each school are assigned to work with these students within their homeroom. The main goal of the resource teacher is to help the students experience

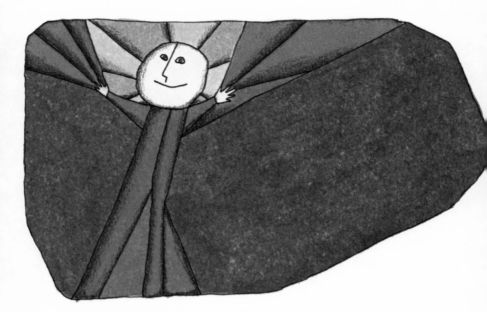

Consider the student as a person, not as a producer.

success in the regular school environment. The teacher travels from room to room, but students stay in the classroom, except for special remedial activities as needed. The resource teacher places greatest emphasis on getting the handicapped or disturbed student in closer positive contact with the others. The traveling teacher sometimes tutors or works in other ways with three or four students within a class—only one of whom may be the student with special problems. At other times, the regular teacher works with a small group while the resource teacher works with the larger group.

Wherever these pioneering efforts are tried, both the academic and social performance of the special students improve. No longer are they separated on the playgrounds of these schools as the "retards" or the "bad kids." As with all new ideas, however, widespread acceptance comes slowly. If such programs are to succeed, staff agreement and involvement are needed as well as cooperative evaluation.

Successful implementation of multi-age, or family grouping of students is going on in schools throughout the country. When teachers in those schools are comfortable with this system, a closer relationship between students and teacher seems to develop. Older students in multi-age classes tend to feel a sense of responsibility for the younger ones, as small tutorial communities are established within the classroom. Teachers of these classes usually become better acquainted with the students, and they concentrate on the uniqueness of each student's learning style instead of being overly concerned with norms.

Continuous progress education (sometimes called individualized, personalized, or open education) is a system by which each student's style and rate of learning is diagnosed, and the information obtained is used to help the student. For this type of education to work successfully, students must be in frequent individual and small group contact with their teacher, tutor, or aide. As these contacts increase, students learn more easily, and loneliness and isolation are reduced.[8]

---

[8] Four basic references for readers interested in continuous progress education and alternative modes of grouping are:

Maurice Gibbons, **Individualized Instruction: A Descriptive Analysis** (Columbia University: Teachers College Press, 1971).

Vincent Rogers, **Teaching in the British Primary** (London: Macmillan & Co., 1970).

Lillian Weber, **The English Infant School and Informal Education** (Englewood Cliffs, New Jersey: Prentice-Hall, 1971).

Bernice Wolfson, **Individualized Instruction** (Encino, California: International Center for Educational Development, 1969).

92

Static ability-grouping, typified by the traditional three reading groups, is being abandoned in some schools as the advantages of more open systems of personalized instruction become apparent. Unhealthy competition and the classification of students into academic pigeonholes are declining as individual development and teacher-student involvement are increasing.

Some precautions are necessary, however, when working in continuous progress learning environments. Teachers who are skilled in using open-education systems often provide a great amount of structure in beginning their work with new classes. Without proper structure, an open environment can cause student frustration and alienation. Many teachers, wishing to be up with the times, moved too rapidly into open forms of education and discovered that they moved too fast for their students. I saw several open-education projects abandoned by well-intentioned teachers when they realized that neither they nor the students were ready for them.[9]

On the other hand, successful teachers practiced open forms of educational involvement long before it became fashionable to do so. The basic ingredients in such openness are respect for each student and the creation of a classroom climate in which success is attainable by all students on their own personal level. Openness is a state of mind. This does not require elaborate planning or special housing and materials, but it does require an attitude on the part of the teacher that each student is important and needs to succeed in school. This type of learning environment based on individual student success within the group can be accomplished without teaming, cooperative teaching, differentiated staffing, or family grouping.

_____

[9] A moving example of the risks involved in opening up the classroom and regrouping may be found in the first chapter of Carl Rogers' work, **Freedom To Learn** (Columbus, Ohio: Charles E. Merrill Co., 1969).

I had the privilege of visiting many classrooms in which an open climate was obviously working. Such classrooms had the following common features:

■ A secure, well-organized, but flexible classroom atmosphere in which each student clearly understood his responsibilities.

■ A trusting attitude of the students toward their peers, as evidenced by their actions with respect to one another.

■ Evidence of careful and cooperative teacher-student planning of learning activities.

■ Fair competition and an emphasis on cooperative group activities[10].

■ Open communication within a businesslike atmosphere.

■ Frequent personal contacts and school-centered conversations between individual students and teacher.

■ Cooperative success activities in which students and teachers participated together, such as games, class projects, trips, discussions, and so on.

True openness, which enables both students and teachers to enjoy school, will develop within such environments.

---

[10] An effective system of cooperative student grouping which is being used successfully is the method of student-support teaming recommended by Gerard A. Poirier in his book, **Students As Partners in Team Learning** (Berkley, California: University of California Press, 1970). This method of enabling students to help each other in class shows promise in reducing isolation and stimulating learning.

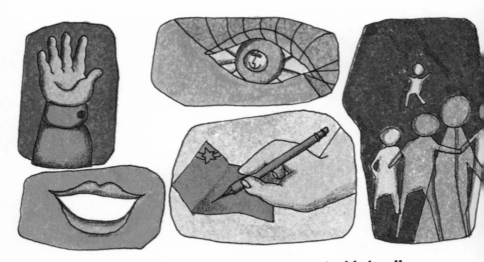

Create a climate in which success is attainable by all students.

HOW CAN YOUR STAFF DEVELOP AND APPLY WAYS OF GROUPING STUDENTS THAT WILL MAKE THEIR LEARNING ENVIRONMENT MORE PERSONALIZED?

WHAT ADDITIONAL IDEAS CAN YOUR STAFF DEVELOP FOR MORE EFFECTIVELY INTEGRATING SPECIAL OR HANDICAPPED STUDENTS INTO THE REGULAR SCHOOL PROGRAM?

DISCUSS TOGETHER THE QUESTION, IN ORDER TO HELP A STUDENT SUCCEED IN SCHOOL, WHAT WOULD BE MOST HELPFUL TO KNOW ABOUT THAT STUDENT?

CAN YOU THINK OF SOME FEASIBLE WAYS TO OPEN UP YOUR CLASSROOM BY USING SOME OF THE IDEAS IN THIS SECTION?

BUILDING PERSONAL INVOLVEMENT AMONG STUDENTS AND TEACHERS

The law makes the child go to school. *Yet unless the school offers something that the student wants or needs, there is*

Building personal involvement among students and teachers.

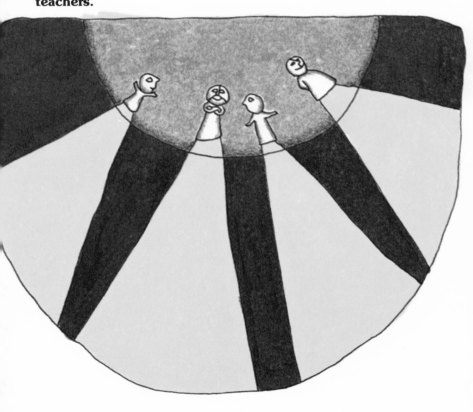

little motivation on his part for either learning or
self-discipline. Whatever causes a student to feel accepted or
happy with himself provides this necessary motivation, and it is
usually based on positive involvement with other persons in the
school. Many excellent teachers with whom I worked showed me
numerous ways of building personal involvement with students
and of constructing success-oriented learning environments within
classrooms and schools.

Some of these success practices are listed below. They indicate
simple yet positive ways of improving the quality of human
relationships between teachers and students. These ideas are
being used successfully at all levels in public and private
schools. They seem to be effective in almost all types of
communities and prove to be well worth the time taken to practice
them.

■ Specific warm and personal teacher actions toward students,
such as eye contact, touching reassuringly, smiling often, calling
students by name, complimenting students on something personal
or some accomplishment, knowing about students' families, using
honest praise, making affirmative verbal contact with each student
in the room at least once a day. One classroom posted as a room
slogan "Smile as you enter."

■ Setting aside a conference time during which students can
discuss whatever is on their mind with the teacher, aides, or other
students. Students sign on the chalkboard for their appointment
time in a responsible manner.

■ Students planning and teaching a lesson to the class in an
area of their special interest or personal expertise.

■ Students being encouraged to write letters and notes to their
teachers and peers. Of course, the teacher must answer.

■ Students from one class visiting another and beginning to break out of the self-contained classroom. Example: In Los Angeles, several kindergarten and first-grade teachers arranged to have their students exchange visits—the kindergarteners to get acquainted with what goes on in the first grade and the first graders to tutor the younger children.

■ Use of Schools Without Failure class meetings[11] to talk about interesting topics and to express opinions in a respectful and nonjudgmental environment. Guests, parents, and resource people who are invited to these meetings often arrange for reciprocal student visits into the community.

■ A suggestion box placed in the classroom in which students can place ideas for classroom improvement and class discussion topics.

■ Students walking to and from the playground with the teacher, instead of lining up. This practice may take a little time to become workable because for years students have been conditioned to form lines.

■ Teachers spending short amounts of time after school with students who *want* to stay.

■ Home contacts by teachers *before* problems develop and sending positive messages to parents when their child does something commendable. Example: A note that was used very effectively stated, *(student's name) did something very good in school today. Please have him tell you about it (teacher's signature).*

---

[11] These class meetings are described in detail in William Glasser's book *Schools Without Failure* (New York: Harper & Row, 1969), Chapters 10, 11, 12.

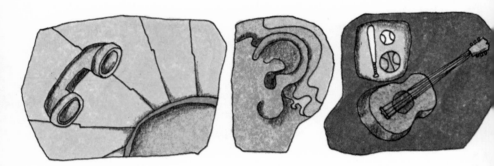

Ways to improve the quality of human relationships in school.

■ Teachers inviting one or more students into their homes or planning and carrying out off-campus activities together.

■ A schoolwide clean-up day during which the principal, entire school staff, and students wear old clothes and scour the school. In one depressed Los Angeles community, parents followed up by painting the entire school.

■ Teachers occasionally parking their cars a block or two from school in the morning and walking to school with the students. Some teachers tried this, and both teachers and students learned a great deal.

■ Developing specific routines to welcome new students to a classroom. These routines are especially useful in transient areas. Class meetings are held to discuss the question, What are the things you would want to know if you were new in this school? Various systems of assigning "buddies" to new students are often used.

■ Teachers occasionally playing on the playground with their classes at recess and at noon—if the teachers have the stamina.

- Teachers eating lunch with their classes in the lunch area once in a while. Some school districts adopt family-style, in-class food-serving programs, with students assuming responsibility for serving and cleaning up.

- Taking students on frequent short walks and trips in the community. This activity pays off since it breaks up the daily routine, relieves classroom tensions, and promotes public relations as the school becomes more visible in the community.

- Sharing photographs of family or baby pictures of both students and teachers. These photos make an interesting and appealing bulletin board.

- A "sunshine call." Teacher telephones parents with a positive comment about their child.

- A very short musical party with bongo drums, guitar, harmonica, and so forth on a student's birthday.

- Using a camera to photograph the citizen of the week and other noteworthy class personnel and activities. The photographs would then be posted.

- Enabling students to arrange material for bulletin boards and for weekly class activity calendars.

- Bringing pets into the classroom. This is a particularly involving activity if the school is located near a housing project in which no pets are allowed.

- Individual and student group interviews in which teachers gather data by asking students how they feel about school. Are they having any problems? If so, what are they? These interviews may also be used to get acquainted with new students, to evaluate programs, and to gather information in order to give special help.

■ The use of creative dramatics and role-playing activities.

■ Improving the makeup of intramural games and physical education. Two or more classes combine to make up teams based on ability levels so that *all* students can play in a fair competitive environment, instead of large groups of students sitting on a bench watching the better players.

■ Teachers socializing with students outside of the classroom at noon, recess, or before and after school.

■ Student-initiated learning activities. These enable students to create and develop class projects, peer-teaching programs, such as special interest days and clubs based on hobbies.

■ Tutoring activities which positively involve students with each other.[12]

■ Maintaining an open-door policy in the morning by allowing students to come into the classroom when they arrive. One school changed its policy from all locked doors in September to all open doors by the end of the school year. The success of this plan was due to the efforts of the teachers, who recognized that it increased their positive involvement with their students and made teaching easier at the cost of a very few minutes each day.

■ Teacher and class writing notes to ill or hospitalized students or teachers.

■ Maintaining contact and involvement with students who move on to a higher grade or to another school.

---

[12] A practical, field-tested tutoring system designed to reduce classroom loneliness and improve reading is described in Elbert H. Ebersole's book, **Programmed Tutoring in Reading** (Pasadena, California: Eberson Enterprises, 1971).

■ Teaching students to work together in groups. Most of the principles of group dynamics that are successful with adults also work with students.

These suggestions for building involvement among teachers and students are only a few among hundreds of success practices being used by teachers all over the United States and Canada. Teachers developed and used these ideas because they found them to be worth the effort. The payoffs are usually greater student motivation to learn and fewer discipline problems—either or both lead to greater professional satisfaction.

HOW COULD SOME OF THESE PRACTICES BE INTRODUCED IN YOUR SCHOOL?

WHAT ARE SOME OTHER WAYS THAT YOUR STAFF FOUND SUCCESSFUL IN DEVELOPING GREATER INVOLVEMENT WITH THEIR STUDENTS AND IN GETTING STUDENTS MORE INVOLVED WITH EACH OTHER?

HOW MANY OF THESE PRACTICES COULD YOU BEGIN IMMEDIATELY?

Almost any teacher asked to choose between teaching a class of thirty-five highly motivated students and a class of fifteen who were unmotivated would choose the former. Most successful teachers view lack of student motivation as the number one learning problem in our schools, and they spend considerable time and effort getting involved with students in order to increase their desire to learn. School districts and educators all over the country are beginning to look at human involvement as it relates to student academic progress.

It is not my purpose to discuss in any detail the art of teaching reading, mathematics, language arts, or other skills and subjects. I assume that the majority of teachers are proficient in teaching basic skills and subject matter. The problem is that many students aren't learning. Few teachers fail because they cannot master the subject matter. Teachers fail or give up because they cannot motivate students to learn. Students who find nothing in school for them feel lonely, uninvolved and, therefore, are unwilling to learn or to do the work required. Sensitive teachers who intuitively recognize this are working in several ways to reduce the separation factors that hinder learning.

LEARNING ABOUT THE STUDENT'S WORLD

Each student comes to school full of experiences which the teacher could use to facilitate learning, but first the teacher must be aware of what these experiences are. This awareness will develop when the teacher finds out what students are doing when they are not in school. Knowing about the student's world in the street, park, and home is essential. Knowing about their economic interests, musical interests, television-viewing habits, toys, transportation, favorite games, and social relationships is also necessary if the teacher is to maintain psychological contact with his class and remain effective.

The easiest way for a teacher to gain this information about the student's world is to ask the student. ***Bringing the student's world into the classroom is the most relevant act a teacher can perform,*** and it pays off in more motivated students. I saw so-called difficult classes positively interacting after several class discussions

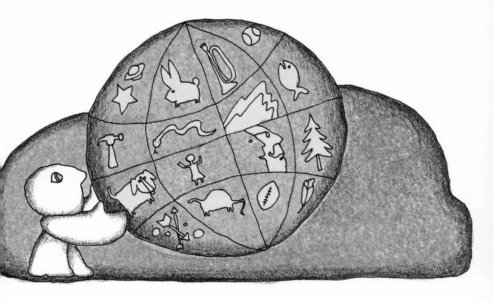

Bringing the student's world into the classroom is the most relevant act a teacher can perform.

on their favorite television programs or on other personal outside interests. Class meetings or discussions on a topic of such unusual student interest as television often lead to many related skill-building activities. Since television is viewed by many students for four to five hours a day—as much time as they spend in school—it seems incredible that the *TV Guide* is not used as a textbook or resource reference in every classroom in the United States.

WHAT ARE SOME WAYS IN WHICH TEACHERS IN YOUR SCHOOL LEARN ABOUT THEIR STUDENTS' WORLDS?

CAN YOUR STAFF EXPERIMENT WITH SOME OF THESE WAYS AND SHARE THEIR EXPERIENCES AND SUCCESSES WITH EACH OTHER?

DIAGNOSING STUDENTS EFFECTIVELY

Teachers who carefully observe their students' behavior and who often talk with them, individually and in small groups, seem to have a far better understanding of student needs than do teachers who rely exclusively on written records and tests. Direct observation of student activity in the class brings the teacher into closer human contact with the student than does the mechanical marking of papers. Observing student behavior patterns provides extremely useful knowledge for the teacher in helping students correct poor learning habits. If time for scheduled observation and subsequent conferencing for each student in the class was built into the schedule at least once every two weeks, the result would be closer teacher-student involvement and greater learning.

When respectful discussion between teacher and class becomes an integral part of the school day, a positive climate is established within which a student is more likely to tell the teacher the real reasons why he is having trouble with spelling or why he can't understand long division problems. *Asking students how they learn skills and subject matter is a technique that is being used effectively by many teachers.* Students can often explain their personally developed learning systems, which can be profitably shared with the class.

Defenses break down as human interaction increases between teacher and student. But this interaction will develop only when the teacher as the adult in charge takes the first step in establishing contact.

WHAT DO YOU FEEL ARE THE MOST EFFECTIVE WAYS TO FIND OUT HOW THE STUDENTS IN YOUR CLASS LEARN AND "WHERE THEY ARE" ON THE LEARNING CONTINUUM OF A PARTICULAR SKILL OR SUBJECT?

CAN YOUR STAFF GET TOGETHER AND SHARE THESE IDEAS? COULD YOU CONSIDER THE POSSIBILITY OF INTERVIEWING SOME STUDENTS AT THESE MEETINGS?

ASKING THE RIGHT QUESTIONS

Since the time of Socrates, mastery of the art of teaching was based on the ability to ask the right questions of ourselves and of others. We learn through inquiry, discussion, and discovery. However, in most of the classrooms that I observe, students are usually asked questions to which there are only right and wrong answers. The questions we deal with in our daily lives are not so simple. What kind of car shall I buy? Can I make this investment with a good chance of realizing a profit? How can I get along better with my mother-in-law or my boss? These questions, which are difficult to answer, represent the kinds of problems faced by us in our daily lives — those requiring high-level thinking operations in order to determine effective courses of action. It is unfortunate that most students do not have the opportunity in school to learn the thinking operations necessary to deal with these kinds of questions.

There are many sources of information that deal with the inquiry process in detail.   My purpose here is only to suggest that there is a place for many kinds of questioning in the classroom. Useful questions could range all the way from "How many is two plus two?" to "What would happen if the North Pole melted this afternoon?" Teachers are finding increasing success in involving and motivating students through more frequent use of open-ended questions.[13]

WHAT KINDS OF QUESTIONS DO YOU ASK OF YOUR STUDENTS EACH DAY?

WHAT KINDS OF QUESTIONS DOES LIFE ASK OF YOU EACH DAY?

HOW MANY OPEN-ENDED QUESTIONS HAVE YOU ASKED THIS WEEK?

CAN YOUR STAFF GET TOGETHER AND PLAN WAYS OF ASKING MORE OPEN-ENDED QUESTIONS IN THEIR CLASSROOMS?

---

[13] Some helpful suggestions for improving the type of questioning that is used in the classroom may be gleaned from the pamphlet entitled, "Teaching Thinking Strategies." Request a copy from the Institute for Staff Development, 3000 Biscayne Boulevard, Suite 316, Miami, Florida 33137.

William Glasser's "Questions for Thinking" also would be helpful. For information on obtaining Dr. Glasser's materials, write to the Educator Training Center, 2401 West Olympic Boulevard, Los Angeles, California 90006.

J. Richard Suchman, Director of Inquiry Training at the University of Illinois in Urbana, also has written material on Inquiry Training.

And, information on the "Far-West Laboratory Mini Courses" may be obtained by contacting the Macmillan Company, Front and Brown Streets, Riverside, New Jersey 08075, or writing to 1 Garden Circle, Hotel Claremont, Berkely, California 94705.

CAN MEMBERS OF THE STAFF GET TOGETHER AND DEVELOP WAYS IN WHICH THESE SKILLS CAN BE BUILT INTO THE CURRICULUM?

DOING SOMETHING ABOUT LISTENING, THINKING, AND SPEAKING

Three skills which probably have the greatest personal, social, and economic payoff in life are listening, thinking, and speaking. Yet a student could conceivably go completely through elementary school and high school without developing them. For some reason these skills were not traditionally considered an important part of most curricula.

In many schools there is no opportunity for a student to learn to speak thoughtfully before his peers in a friendly, accepting environment. Sometimes students are required to stand before a class and read a prepared report or recite a poem, but this is not conducive to developing the skills of "thinking on your feet" or extemporaneously dealing with problems through dialogue.

In *How Children Fail,* John Holt describes the true test of intelligence or thinking as deciding what to do when we don't know what to do. When faced with such a decision we must use our higher thought processes such as analysis, synthesis, and evaluation. Why not set up the school environment so that more of this kind of thinking is stimulated? Even very young children can improve their thinking skills as they solve relevant problems in class. Great pleasure is experienced by students who use their minds in such ways.

Skillful teachers are continuing to increase the opportunities for listening, thinking, and speaking experiences in the classroom. Such methods are:

■ Providing time for students to talk about relevant topics in a structured but nonjudgmental environment.

■ Encouraging students to orally describe their experiences and interests before their peers.

■ Asking students the kinds of questions which promote the use of higher thought processes.

■ Encouraging students to discuss their opinions and questioning students about those opinions until essential meanings are reached.

■ Encouraging students to question and challenge each other in respectful and nonthreatening ways.

■ Providing opportunities for students to learn how to handle unfamiliar situations and emergencies.

■ Enabling students to teach each other and to make group presentations before the class.

- Allowing students to deal with physical and mechanical problems (such as bicycle repair) that they may confront outside of school.

- Arranging for debates and panel discussions.

- Inviting guests and resource people into class to be interviewed by students.

As these kinds of activities and processes become a part of the learning environment in schools and classrooms, students and teachers will increase their positive involvement with each other and with the curriculum. Loneliness and separation will be reduced.

HOW CAN SOME OF THESE SUGGESTIONS BE INITIATED IN YOUR SCHOOL?

IN WHAT WAYS HAVE YOU ENCOURAGED STUDENTS TO USE LISTENING, THINKING, AND SPEAKING SKILLS IN YOUR SCHOOL OR CLASSROOM?

REALISTIC REPORTING TO PARENTS AND STUDENTS

As long as parents feel a strong need to know how their children are doing in school, there is little probability that reporting systems will be discontinued. However, increasing dissatisfaction with traditional report cards has prompted searches for more meaningful alternatives.

A-B-C-D-F and 1-2-3-4-5 marking systems are losing credibility as both parents and teachers recognize that such procedures are inaccurate, unrealistic, and therefore, severely limited as evaluative tools. In addition, they are almost always negative in their effect on students; they are instrumental in promoting feelings of failure; and they have little educational value.

The strong emphasis placed on marks often encourages cheating and other undesirable practices, as well as placing a ceiling on the performance of many high-ability students. Questions such as, "Will this be on the test?" and "What do I have to do to get an *A*?" are indications that students are limiting their efforts to the constraints of the marking mechanism. This system severely limits the teacher's responsibility in really examining student performance in a constructive and meaningful way. A *C* mark could be given to a student, even though the teacher may have little understanding of that student's true performance or potential. The meaninglessness of letter grades frustrates conscientious teachers as they unhappily attempt to standardize their values within the school.

The reporting system which I believe holds the most promise for bringing student, teacher, and parents together in positive and productive ways is **the student-centered three-way conference.** This conference is a discussion between the teacher and the student, with the parents as participating observers. The main focus of the dialogue is on the student's accomplishment and commitment to continuous progress and improvement.

The basic advantage of such a system is that the student becomes the prime contractor for his education; he assumes some responsibility instead of being a pawn in the reporting process between parents and teacher.

Development and organization of three-way conferences must be planned carefully. I outlined some sequential procedures being

**The student-centered three-way conference holds the
most promise.**

used by schools which are having success with this method of
reporting. These steps are general suggestions to be adapted to
the special needs of participating school communities.

Step I

The school staff holds several meetings to discuss the advantages
and disadvantages of three-way conferencing. Topical questions
to consider might be: How to motivate students without using the
grading system? How to assess community readiness? How to find

the time and the mechanics of implementing conferences? How to develop skill in conducting conferences? Time is allowed for teacher reaction and research. Since many teachers have strong opinions about student reporting and some may have had direct experience with conferences, ample time should be allowed for thorough exploration of all facets of the conference process. Information may be sought from schools which have experience in using three-way conferences.[14]

Step II

The staff and community meet together. Parent Advisory Councils, the PTA, and representative staff members discuss how the community views student reporting and whether or not parents are receptive to the idea of the three-way conference. Since many parents have a strong attachment to the report card system, stress must be placed on the *improvement of the reporting procedure rather than on the elimination of the report card.*

Step III

If the staff and community agree on the desirability of introducing three-way conferences, plans should be made to organize faculty meetings by grade level to discuss the specifics of the process. Trial conferences by selected teachers could be held and later discussed at these meetings. Students are brought into special staff meetings for the purpose of practicing conference procedures. Each level of the faculty develops its own plan for conferencing but

---

[14] A listing of many of the schools in the United States which have experience with the student, teacher, parent conference is available through The Program Director, Educator Training Center, 2140 W. Olympic Blvd., Los Angeles, California 90006.

must keep within the general guidelines developed by the entire staff. Points to consider in organizing the conferences are:

- How to keep conference records.

- How to follow-up on student commitments.

- Providing the time required for effective conferencing. Since conferencing is far more time consuming than the report card system, release time for teachers is essential if this system of reporting is to be developed effectively.

- Clarifying the roles and responsibilities of the student, teacher, and parent in the conference.

- Initiating the three-way conference. Some schools elect to incorporate conferences into one or two grade levels each year; other schools implement conferences at all grade levels in the same year. Each school-community must decide for itself.

- How to handle parents who are dissatisfied with the conferences. A successful course of action is to offer any dissatisfied parent the traditional report card in place of the conference. Generally, those parents who choose the former soon recognize the superiority of the three-way conference as a reporting process.

Step IV

The conference plan is put into operation. As it develops, small groups of teachers should meet frequently to discuss progress and refine techniques.

Step V

Teachers, students, and parents should be asked their opinion of the ongoing conference procedures. What went well? What could be improved? In some schools, parents are asked these questions immediately following the conferences. All reasonable suggestions for improving the conference system should be considered, adopted, if possible, and publicized within the school community.

The three-way conference procedure may be difficult to initiate as teachers, parents, and students have been conditioned to traditional report cards and may be reluctant to let them go. Where conferences are positively and enthusiastically initiated by teachers, conditions which reduce separation among teachers, students, and parents develop. Some examples are:

- Students develop a deeper knowledge of their strengths and weaknesses and accept more responsibility for their own learning.

- Teachers acquire a greater awareness of their students' individual learning rates and styles. As a result of conferencing, involvement between student and teacher increases.

- Teachers develop a closer and more positive relationship with parents. Their contacts become more personal and productive.

- Positive parental involvement with the school increases. Parents feel closer to the school. The conference seems to be a subtle and effective form of parent education.

- Teachers note a follow-through on most commitments made by students in conferences. This opportunity for student responsibility did not exist when report cards were used.

**ARE YOU SATISFIED WITH THE STUDENT PROGRESS
REPORTING SYSTEM IN YOUR SCHOOL? IS IT
REALISTIC? DOES IT MOTIVATE AND ENCOURAGE
STUDENTS TO LEARN?**

**CAN YOUR STAFF CONSIDER INTRODUCING MORE
PERSONAL AND PRODUCTIVE FORMS OF
STUDENT REPORTING?**

**CAN YOU SEE ANY PROFESSIONAL PAYOFF IN
ADOPTING THE THREE-WAY CONFERENCE?**

**IN WHAT WAYS COULD YOU ARRANGE FOR RELEASE
TIME IN YOUR SCHOOL FOR THE PURPOSE OF
PLANNING AND HOLDING CONFERENCES?**

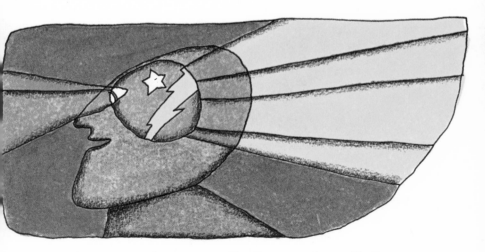

**Teachers are seeking more effective ways to motivate
students.**

RESPONSIBLE BEHAVIOR AND SELF-DISCIPLINE

In spite of all we know about human behavior, we traditionally used punishment expediently in the hope of developing an orderly school with highly motivated learners. That punishment does not work is becoming increasingly evident, and teachers are beginning to seek more effective ways of motivating students.

For years experts in human behavior have suggested ways to help students learn how to behave responsibly. Yet it is only recently, as problems in the schools are becoming monumental and as corporal punishment is beginning to be eliminated by statute, that these experts are getting a hearing. I find that those methods which are both nonpunitive and nonpermissive have the greatest chance for success with today's learners.

The system with which I have had personal experience and success during the past several years is William Glasser's reality therapy model. This model, extensively and successfully field tested, incorporates the following practical ideas for developing a total school approach to discipline.

■ School should be an enjoyable place for students. Students should *want* to be in school. School should be a place where students can use their minds to learn necessary skills and to deal with relevant issues. It should be a place with warm, caring human persons who are capable of involvement. Unless school is such a place, there is no point in worrying about discipline. If the students don't want to be there, and if they are there only because the law says that they must be, then we have the preconditions of a power struggle in which no one will win. Therefore, most school staff efforts should be directed toward developing a successful school environment in which students *want* to be. It is hoped that some of the suggestions in this book will help in planning such an environment.

■ Students should have a real knowledge of the rules. Rules should be reasonable. They should be explained and discussed thoroughly. Example: Most students can easily recite the school rules, especially the one about no running in the halls. Yet students find little rationale for this rule; therefore, it is usually unenforceable, and running in the halls and corridors persists. School-wide discussion of rules should be encouraged to reduce the number of rules to the minimum necessary in effectively running the school.

■ Students should be involved in the rule-making process. Both in the classroom and in the school, rules which are no longer useful or practical should be changed or eliminated.

■ Something should happen when rules are broken. If the sanctions are understood and agreed upon, their enforcement is not punitive. Natural and logical consequences are not punitive. The enforcement of just rules should teach improved ways of behaving and should increase the student's involvement with school.

Corporal punishment and suspension, which are sometimes necessary courses of action, are expedient behavior control techniques. However, these methods do not usually produce any lasting or positive behavioral change since they further isolate the student and aggravate the problem, as responsibility passes from the student to the adult.

Punishment and permissiveness are the twin detractors of responsible behavior in the schools. Each is an example of the easy way out. Rage and frustration are demonstrated by punishment. Lack of concern is illustrated by permissiveness.

If all of these steps can become operational in your school, ask your students the following reality therapy questions in order to maintain your involvement and to begin teaching students better ways to act responsibly.[15]

■ What did you do? This establishes the circumstances of the situation and clarifies the student's responsibility.

■ Did it help you? The student evaluates his own actions. Also, if there is a good relationship between the teacher and student, the underlying assumption will be that I (the teacher) believe that you can be responsible for your life.

■ Can you make a plan? Can we (teacher and student) make a plan together? A plan should be developed that the student can carry out. It should be simple enough that success and self-worth will be assured. It should involve action (I will change my seat) rather than nonaction (I will stop bothering Johnny).

■ Will you carry out the plan? This illustrates the student's commitment to the plan. The commitment is only as good as the involvement with the person to whom he makes the commitment.

■ Did you do what you said you would do? Did the student keep his commitment? If he did not, accept no excuses, but do not punish him. Substitute sensible sanctions and logical

---

[15] For more information about reality therapy, consult William Glasser's books, *Reality Therapy* (New York: Harper & Row, 1965) *and Schools Without Failure* (New York: Harper & Row, 1969). Also see Rudolf Dreikurs', *Psychology in the Classroom* (New York: Harper & Row, 1957). This book includes many helpful examples of logical and natural consequences.

consequences instead of punishment. Keep using this method of planning and commitment until the student's behavior improves, and when it does, reinforce it.

DOES YOUR SCHOOL HAVE A DISCIPLINE POLICY? WHAT IS IT? IS IT PRACTICAL?

DOES YOUR STAFF AGREE ON THE BASIC DEFINITIONS OF THE WORDS: DISCIPLINE, PUNISHMENT, AND RESPONSIBLE BEHAVIOR?

IS THE FOCUS OF DISCIPLINE IN YOUR SCHOOL ON TEACHING BETTER WAYS OF BEHAVING? IS IT WORKING?

DO YOU THINK THAT YOU WOULD BE WILLING TO DISCUSS AND POSSIBLY USE THESE METHODS IN CONJUNCTION WITH OTHER MEMBERS OF YOUR SCHOOL STAFF?

HOW COULD PARENTS IN YOUR SCHOOL COMMUNITY WORK WITH THE SCHOOL STAFF IN HELPING TO BUILD RESPONSIBLE BEHAVIOR IN STUDENTS?

These suggestions for getting teachers and students together were tried in many places. They worked successfully and are yours to try if you think they will help in your school. Reducing the separation and loneliness factors among teachers and students can only take place, however, if plans are made by the staff to actively work for a friendlier and more involved school environment.

GETTING SCHOOL STAFFS

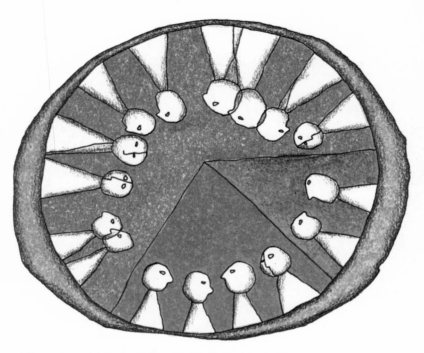

There is a real need for staffs to get together.

In Chapters 4 and 5, I identified what I believe to be the basic factors that prevent school staffs from working closely together. It is not enough, however, to know what is wrong. Action must be taken to change or eliminate these factors so that more staff members can get involved with each other in experiencing personal and professional satisfaction.

Overcoming these separators requires that ways be developed for creatively using professional time, meeting more effectively, opening up the school for adults, creating a climate of trust, and dealing with the changing relationships between school administrators and faculty members. School staffs which increase their involvement and reduce professional loneliness actively and directly deal with these separators by using some of the following ideas.

FINDING TIME TO GET TOGETHER

Unless school staffs can find meeting time to solve problems and to develop successful programs, they lose their effectiveness as an educational unit. Time to meet under professionally rewarding conditions is the most critical element in the success or failure of a faculty but remains the commodity in shortest supply in schools today.

Because of years of frustration with and negative reactions to the traditional one-way communication sessions that passed for faculty meetings, teachers are not overjoyed at the prospect of seeking out time to meet in the school setting. Yet there is a very real need for staffs to get together in small and large groups to discuss the problems and plans that will influence their professional lives.

The first part of the problem then is *a desire to meet.* Desire is strongly associated with engagment in activities that bring the participants success and a feeling of self-worth. Teachers and principals need to cooperate and plan together if successful and effective interaction is to take place on a continuing basis. This successful interaction will only happen when administrative trivia is relegated to bulletins and when staff meetings become professional seminars in which student-related issues, such as learning, motivation, and responsible behavior are discussed and dealt with. As faculties begin to realize that they can successfully cope with their problems, they will make time to get together.

The second part of the problem is *when and how to meet.* Before teachers become motivated enough to meet on their own time, much creative attention needs to be directed toward finding ways of enabling staffs to get together on school time. Obviously, teachers do not relish meeting at the end of a hard day. Few if any useful school programs are developed by faculties after school. Even though teachers don't have the requisite amount of energy at the end of the day, we persist with the traditional afternoon faculty meeting because we've always done it that way.

The following ideas are being used in many schools, and they are offered here as a few among many possible alternatives to the old-time patterns for staff communication. They may be modified according to school-community needs and resources.

Early and Short Meetings

Try scheduling short meetings in the morning, one-half to three-quarters of an hour before school begins. In this way, prompt termination of the meeting is assured. Furthermore, ideas and plans under discussion during the meeting may be tried out during the day while they are still in mind. I talked to many faculties who feel that one-half hour in the morning is more effective than one hour after school. Lunchtime meetings are also successful if used infrequently. If such meetings are to be successful, it is necessary to obtain a commitment from participants to start on time and to follow an agenda, usually limited to one or two topics.

Primary-Grade/Upper-Grade Cooperation

In many schools, kindergarten and primary teachers send their classes home approximately one hour before the intermediate or upper grades leave school. These primary teachers are sometimes willing to take over upper-grade classrooms in order to give their colleagues an occasional opportunity to meet on school time. Upper-grade teachers can return the favor by sending older students to serve and help as tutors in the lower grades. This type of arrangement has the additional advantage of increasing professional contact between teachers who do not normally interact with one another.

District Release Time

In many districts, professional student free days are scheduled once a month or more. During such times, useful in-service training is planned for the day, and local school problems may be dealt with in unhurried and productive ways. The value of such meetings is being increasingly recognized as a positive step toward the solution of proliferating educational problems. If your school district does not provide student free time, teacher organizations, administrator organizations, parents' groups and others interested in school improvement should survey the possibilities of such an in-service arrangement and make their views known to the local board of education.

Credit Classes

Many teachers working for incentive credit, renewal of credential credit, or in-service points may avail themselves of district-sponsored classes, from which they will receive professional rewards for their time and effort. Many such classes and seminars designed by school districts, colleges, or reputable private educational consulting firms are organized so that teachers have time to plan practical solutions to local school problems within the scope of their in-service training. An example of such a system is the Schools Without Failure Program, which is co-sponsored by the Educator Training Center in Los Angeles, California and La Verne College. This program is operating in hundreds of schools throughout the United States.

Relief by Support Personnel

Release time for small groups of teachers who need time to

meet together can be arranged by combining the classes of those teachers for auditorium and special programs, films, or play days under the supervision of an administrator, school nurse, counselor, aide, or other available auxiliary personnel. Sometimes several parent volunteers under the direction of an administrator or teacher can assume responsibility for supervision of released teachers' classes. Arranging release time in these ways has two important side benefits. First, it lets the released teachers know that professional meeting time is valuable enough to warrant special scheduling. Second, it enables administrators, counselors, nurses, and other nonteaching personnel to regain educational credibility with teachers as they work directly with students in the classroom.

Professional Social Meetings

Combining professional/social meetings is successful in many schools. Picnics, Friday afternoon socials, or any special occasion get-togethers are often pleasant ways to conduct a modicum of business in relaxed surroundings. As a faculty becomes more close-knit, there will be less distinction drawn between the social and professional aspects of the job.

Use of Funds

Whenever available, special state, local, or federal funds may be used to buy substitute teacher time for the release of teachers. Some school districts employ ESEA Title I monies for in-service training release time during the school day, when teacher receptivity and productivity are optimum. Sometimes these funds are also used to compensate teachers for attending meetings that are held during nonteaching time.

Schedule Adjustments

Many types of schedule adjustments are made by schools in setting aside some school time for faculty interaction. Several

When was the last time you were determined to do something to make a difference?

school districts begin the school day ten minutes early and cut down on lunchtime, thereby gaining enough time to send the students home early one afternoon each week. These afternoons may be spent in professional interaction. The successful operation of these plans is limited only by negotiation agreements, legal considerations, community opinion, and the creativity of the staff.

128

Special Permission

As school districts recognize the need for staff development, some school boards grant permission on an experimental basis for faculties to meet on school time. Carefully thought-out plans for use of professional time when presented by a local staff to upper-level administrators and to school boards often receive budgetary support for providing release time.

ARE YOUR STAFF MEETINGS HELD AFTER SCHOOL ACCORDING TO TRADITIONAL PATTERNS? ARE THE MEETINGS USUALLY PRODUCTIVE AND EFFECTIVE? HOW DOES YOUR STAFF EVALUATE THESE MEETINGS? ARE THERE PROFESSIONAL OR MATERIAL REWARDS FOR STAFF MEMBERS WHO ATTEND THE MEETINGS?

COULD YOUR STAFF EXPLORE WAYS OF FINDING ALTERNATIVE TIMES FOR HOLDING LARGE AND SMALL GROUP STAFF MEETINGS? CONSIDER SOME OF THE SUGGESTIONS IN THIS SECTION. WOULD YOU BE WILLING TO EXPERIMENT WITH SOME OF THE IDEAS MENTIONED?

IN WHAT ADDITIONAL WAYS COULD YOU FIND "PRIME TIME" FOR PROFESSIONAL COMMUNICATION?

MEETING TOGETHER EFFECTIVELY

Having examined some ways of finding time to meet together, let's look at what can be done to make meetings work more effectively.

When was the last time that you attended a meeting and walked away with a real sense of purpose, determined to really do something to make a difference? If you felt that way, chances are you contributed successfully as a respected member of the group. This kind of a feeling is more likely to flourish when certain separation-reducing factors are present to assure involvement and success. *These factors are not complicated to understand,* although they have been the topics of many articles, books, and manuals. In some districts, expensive human relations training courses are offered and consultants are hired to help manage school meetings in order to achieve desired goals. Unfortunately, the average school staff has neither the time to read through the volumes of material nor the access to expensive training services. Therefore, several basic techniques for increasing involvement and improving interaction in school staff meetings are listed and briefly explained below. These suggestions are being used successfully in many schools.

Furniture Arrangement

When the furniture is arranged so that all participants can see one another, more effective communication takes place. Furniture should be arranged at faculty meetings with the same thought in mind as it is in the classroom—to bring people together. A circular formation is usually the most conducive to conversation. The traditional one-way speaker-to-audience communication arrangement is effective only when the speaker has not planned for audience interaction, when he has something of critical importance to say, or when he has great charisma and speaking ability.

Place of Meeting

The assurance of successful and productive meetings depends to a great extent on where they are held. If you have ever participated in a retreat or a conference among the pines or at

the beach, you probably remember feeling happy about whatever
it was that went on there. School auditoriums, classrooms, and
most faculty lounges, on the other hand, leave a great deal to
be desired in terms of the ideal setting for professional interaction.
It would be unrealistic to recommend planning elaborate
surroundings for all staff meetings, yet many school faculties
leave the school grounds almost routinely for their meetings.
Teachers and parents who live close to the school are often
willing to open their homes to the staff. An occasional meeting
in a hotel or restaurant also helps change the pace. People seem
closer and more comfortable away from school for several
reasons, not the least of which is the opportunity to sit in a
soft chair.

Simple Group Dynamics

If dull and unproductive meetings are to be avoided, meetings
should be held within alternating large and small groups. When
large groups are used over prolonged periods of time, they are
threatening and stupefying. Small groups enable more people
to talk and focus on concrete problems. Assigning a problem to
several small groups who then bring suggested solutions back
to the large group is a far better use of brain power than attempting
to get consensus in a large group. It's that simple. Yet in schools
all over the country why do we fail to break up our large meetings
in order to process ideas more effectively? Why not take advantage
of the large group to small group and back to large group system
which is a basic group dynamics technique successfully used for
years in the field of business?

Sharing Meeting Leadership

As many members of the staff as feasible should be involved in
planning the meeting agenda and in sharing responsibility for
leading discussions. Without this sharing, one-way communication
generally takes place and the administrator is forced into the role

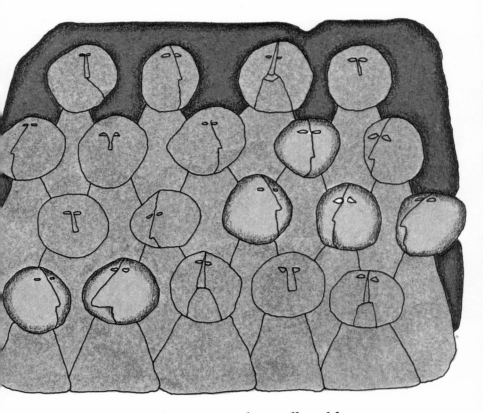

Small groups enable more people to talk and focus on concrete problems.

of the paternalistic answer man. An effective way to encourage shared leadership is to ask faculty members to submit short written evaluations of their meetings. Most teachers like to be asked their opinions and through occasional simple evaluations may identify certain aspects of staff meetings that could be improved. This evaluation process will involve teachers in the improvement of their own meetings, and it may encourage teachers to assume greater responsibility for planning and leadership.

The Positive Approach

Begin each meeting on a positive note. Focus on a successful follow-through from a previous meeting, on a breakthrough in a particular problem, or on a personal success experience by a staff member. This type of approach will set the tone of a meeting and will help to avoid the traditional litany of grievances so customary at faculty meetings. Although an occasional gripe session is necessary and helps relieve tension, there is greater payoff for all through a continual focus on school problems and an accompanying search for positive solutions. This approach will encourage teachers to direct their hostility against problems instead of people.

It is particularly important for staff members to reinforce each other by pointing out small increments of success, *since positive progress in schools is slow and difficult to identify.* Without some awareness of successes, however small, teachers become discouraged and alienated and the quality of meetings often deteriorates.

Pacing Meetings

Sitting in one place for over half an hour can be quite painful unless one is extremely motivated. This is why so many teachers knit their way through faculty meetings and manage to remain totally uninvolved. This type of alienation may be avoided by using varying modes of presentation such as films, tapes, other media, and small group discussions. Frequent stretch breaks also help. Another surefire way of brightening up staff meetings is to occasionally invite groups of students in to give their views on the problem under consideration. Valuable data may be obtained as staff members interact with students in a nonclassroom environment.

Combination Meetings and "Experts"

It is a good idea to occasionally schedule a joint meeting with another school. Common problems can be discussed, new friendships are formed, and professional growth is encouraged as teachers share experiences and ideas with each other. Teachers should routinely be invited to share their expertise with other faculties. Invite administrators or other community-minded individuals from different areas, who will act as resource people or "experts" in your school. Business has long recognized the value of the outside consultant. Educators should use the many qualified people in their own ranks to help them grow professionally.

Follow-Through

A common complaint about staff meetings is that participants usually come back to meetings feeling the same way they did the week before. A meeting should not be concluded without deciding who is going to do what before the next meeting. There should be a feeling that all meetings are connected with each other so that staff members can feel the sense of progress and accomplishment so necessary to group morale.

Getting Agreement

Although solutions to school problems can't often be found and wrapped up neatly at the end of each meeting, staff members must keep talking, or they will never reach a consensus. This is not easy, particularly in the pressure-cooker environment of our schools. Staff members sometime feel like giving up and rushing to a vote before adequately discussing a topic, or alternatively, letting someone else make the decision. These recourses are both dead ends which rarely help solve problems and which ultimately weaken the group. Staff members need to keep talking through their problems in both large and small groups until all are in

Staff members need to talk through their problems.

agreement with some part of the proposed solutions. When at least partial agreement is reached, separation is reduced and more progress made possible.

These suggestions for improving faculty meetings are certainly not classified information. They have been used by skillful group leaders in business and industry for years with great success. Surprisingly, however, they are not often used in the schools. Although the ideas are simple and effective, they are difficult to introduce because they fly in the face of musty tradition.

Teachers and administrators who adopt these techniques almost always improve the professional communication in their schools and develop even better ideas of their own.

**HOW WOULD YOU DESCRIBE THE KINDS OF STAFF
MEETINGS THAT TAKE PLACE IN YOUR SCHOOL?
DO THEY BRING PEOPLE TOGETHER OR DO THEY
KEEP PEOPLE APART?**

**COULD YOUR STAFF AGREE TO INITIATE SOME OF THE
SUGGESTIONS MENTIONED IN THIS SECTION? COULD
YOU DEVELOP AND ORGANIZE YOUR OWN MEETING
IMPROVEMENT PLAN, WITH THE GOAL OF BRINGING
STAFF MEMBERS CLOSER TOGETHER?**

BUILDING A CLIMATE OF TRUST AND INVOLVEMENT

There are survey instruments that are specifically designed to
measure the human relations climate in schools, but most
perceptive substitute teachers can gain fairly accurate assessment
of a school's personality well before their first day's work has
ended.[16] Indeed, parents, bus drivers, counselors, and almost
anyone else who has spent much time in and around schools can
intuitively sense the quality of the relationships among staff
members by observing certain actions within the school. To name
a few: Do students act in friendly ways toward teachers and other
adults? How is a visitor received in the faculty lounge or in the
office? How is a student received in the faculty lounge? What is the
nature of the interaction among staff members on school grounds
and in the faculty room? Do teachers talk positively about students,
parents, and each other most of the time?

---

[16] The most popular and useful of these is the Organizational Climate
Description Questionnaire developed by Andrew W. Halpin and Don B.
Croft in their book, *The Organizational Climate of Schools* (Chicago:
University of Chicago Press, 1963).

If the answers to these and related questions indicate a lack of trust and positive involvement among staff members, specific steps must be taken to encourage contact and to develop human-support systems in the school environment. Without direct action, nothing will change, and as outside political and community pressures increase, staff relationships will deteriorate.

The following are a few ideas and strategies that are being successfully applied as principals and teachers work toward the difficult task of developing trust and involvement in their educational communities.

ESTABLISHING CONTACT

The need for staff members to establish positive personal and professional contact with each other is critical to the development of a healthy school climate for students as well as for the adults who work there. Lack of contact is an unspoken and unresolved problem in too many schools. Not enough time is spent working out specific ways of increasing positive staff interaction because it is sometimes too painful to examine our own professional behavior. When staffs begin to look at what they are doing, however, good things can happen. This is illustrated by describing an experience which has been repeated in several schools.

School X was suffering the usual headaches common to many schools today, such as low reading scores, parental pressures, student discipline problems, and accountability demands. Several demoralizing meetings were held during which all of the frustrations and seemingly unsolvable school problems were resurrected and fruitlessly discussed. The tone of the dialogue was shrill, argumentative, and generally reflective of the tensions of the times. When the group was asked questions as, "What are we doing here?" and "Are we solving any problems?" the teachers came to a gradual realization of their basic difficulty—to quote Pogo, "We have met the enemy, and they are us." They realized that no problems would be solved and no consensus reached until they could begin getting together in more friendly and more respectful ways. Cooperative decisions were made to begin communicating on a personal/social level before getting into the more difficult professional areas. At this point the social committee came into operation with no objective other than to get *all* the members of the staff together in pleasant, comfortable, and nonthreatening surroundings.[17] Persistent efforts were necessary to contact and obtain commitment for attendance from *each* staff member. The committee reached out to even the most defensive and isolated staff members. ***This reach out is critical.*** It doesn't matter whether the staff gets together on or off the school grounds or whether they meet in the morning, afternoon, or evening. It is only important that everyone attend. In some schools, it may be the first time teachers have ever come together socially. This initial contact should be short and pleasant so that everyone will want to repeat the experience.

As staff members relax and feel comfortable with each other on a personal level—and this may take a year or more of effort and planning—various strategies may be attempted to maintain the positive contacts. Several ideas which are being practiced successfully are:

■ Sign-up potluck lunches or "salad days" once a month at which teachers take turns contributing food.

---

[17] In schools where positive climates exist, the social committee or its equivalent usually plays an important role. It is more than a group that plans parties, arranges for wedding gifts, and baby showers. The members of an effective social committee are respected members of the staff who recognize that their function contributes significantly to the quality of professional as well as to social interaction on the part of the staff.

Get the staff together in pleasant, nonthreatening surroundings.

■ Impromptu birthday parties after school or at break times.

■ A Friday afternoon (TGIF) group which meets off school grounds on a regular basis.

■ Faculty meetings held off school grounds.

■ Luncheons held off school grounds once a month.

■ Rescheduled recesses and lunch periods in large schools in order to enable teachers to have contact at break times with each other that they ordinarily do not have. Problems often develop due to the usual separation of primary and upper-grade teachers at these times.

■ An invitation to the staff for a social function at the home of the principal. These seem to be well attended.

■ A picnic, barbecue, or some other type of "family" get-together for the staff once or twice a year.

■ Lunch or breakfast served to the staff by students, who should be assisted the first time by the social committee.

■ Progressive dinners in staff members' homes—one course at each residence.

■ Professional exchange day. All teaching assignments, including those of principal and assistant principal, are written on cards and placed in a box. Each staff member draws a different assignment for one day or one hour. The follow-through on this activity takes a little courage, but pays off in increased staff contact and mutual respect.

■ Traditional or seasonal parties held either before or after the particular season, when staff members are more relaxed.

■ A "Secret Santa." During the week before Christmas vacation, each staff member draws the name of another. Keeping their anonymity, positive notes and messages are placed each day in the mailbox of the person whose name was drawn. After a week of these positive messages, identities are revealed at a Friday get-together. This activity may be adapted to any time of the year.

■ Punch or coffee served in the office on Friday afternoon as teachers get together for some conversation before going home.

Any school can adapt these ideas to its local needs or develop its own plans for increasing positive personal/social contact among teachers. ***The important point is that someone on the staff must initiate and coordinate efforts in these directions.*** The question is, Who? The answer to that question will vary from school to school. In some schools it will be an administrator; in others, a respected teacher, a social committee, or perhaps the school secretary. It is hoped that by reading and then discussing the ideas on these pages, someone will begin the process of moving toward improved human contact in the school.

Another contributor to professional loneliness is the clique. Cliques may develop for a variety of reasons, such as differences in interests between new and experienced teachers or between organization members and nonmembers. The kind of clique a teacher joins may depend on which department he is in, which grade level he teaches, his political persuasions, or personal/social considerations. In any case, cliques are often divisive and must be dealt with if an effective learning climate is to be developed and maintained.

The negative effect of in-groups and out-groups based on personal or professional bias may be mitigated through the efforts of concerned individuals or groups on the staff—though there is no proved or tested working procedure for handling such conflicts. Strategies for bringing teachers together will vary from school to school. The negative effect of some cliques may sometimes be offset by planned efforts to involve members of out-groups in success-directed activities with other members of the staff.

Reaching out to out-groups, however, must be thoughtfully organized. Who does what needs to be planned in advance. For example: Who would be the logical person to take Mrs. X, the grand dragon of the kindergarten primary department, out to lunch in order to encourage her participation and support for the new staff development seminars? Who will extend personal invitations to the three new teachers who always eat lunch by themselves to join the group next Thursday? Which teacher on the staff might be able to act as liaison between the leaders of the militant and conservative teachers before the next staff meeting? These and similar separation problems are not easy to solve, but if staff members can begin planning specific ways of moving toward instead of away from self-isolating groups, contact may be established and productive dialogue begun.

When all reach out efforts to cliques have failed, a realistic choice must be made. Either the staff must learn to live with and work around the problems caused by the cliques, or direct administrative intervention will be required if personal conflicts directly affect the learning environment of the students.

Grade-level and departmental clannishness has been handled by organizing **cross grade-level or interdepartmental planning teams,** the members of which work together in areas of general concern, such as discipline, counseling, assessment, and school organization. Such teams are composed of representatives from each grade level or department. The members work to improve communication within the school and to supplement grade-level committees. But more important, when teachers of kindergarten through grade six and special education or various departments meet together in small planning groups, traditional conflicts seem to be reduced as greater insight is gained into each others' problems.

In addition to these suggestions for establishing contact among staff members, there are many field-tested experiences specifically designed to increase and improve human interaction. Although some of these experiences are gamelike and contrived, they

142

nevertheless work—many faculties dramatically improve the relationships among their members through their use.[18]

For a variety of reasons, staff relations in some schools may become extremely strained, if not fractured. When there seem to be irreconcilable differences among staff members, it helps for an outside person to come into the school in order to facilitate staff communication and to ease tensions. The less threatening and more objective role of the outside consultant in defusing difficult situations is well established in the behavioral sciences. It is not necessary that these outside "experts" come from expensive consulting firms. Many school districts have among their own personnel, resource people who are qualified to serve in this capacity. I have seen teachers and principals work effectively with faculties other than their own in helping to improve deteriorating staff relations. Educators should make greater use of their own local "experts," some of whom are far more valuable and credible than costly out-of-district resource people.

HOW WOULD YOU ASSESS YOUR SCHOOL'S HUMAN RELATIONS CLIMATE? IS IT FRIENDLY? WHAT IS THE NATURE OF THE CONTACT AMONG THE STAFF MEMBERS?

---

[18] For ideas in using group experiences to improve human relations climate consider selections from the following:

J. William Pfeiffer and John E. Jones, *A Handbook of Structured Experiences for Human Relations Training* (Iowa City, Iowa: University Associates Publishers and Consultants, 1969).

Sidney J. Parnes, *Creative Behavior Materials* (New York: Charles Scribner & Sons, 1967).

Louis Raths, Merrill Harmin and Sidney B. Simon, *Values and Teaching* (Columbus, Ohio, Charles E. Merrill, 1966).

IS YOUR SCHOOL'S SOCIAL COMMITTEE EFFECTIVE IN
KEEPING *ALL* MEMBERS OF THE STAFF IN CONTACT
WITH EACH OTHER? WHAT IS DONE TO BREAK DOWN
ANY ISOLATING OR DESTRUCTIVE CLIQUES IN YOUR
SCHOOL?

WOULD YOUR STAFF BE WILLING TO ATTEMPT SOME
OF THE CONTACT STRATEGIES DESCRIBED? WHAT
CONTACT STRATEGIES COULD BE DEVELOPED TO
MEET THE NEEDS OF YOUR SCHOOL?

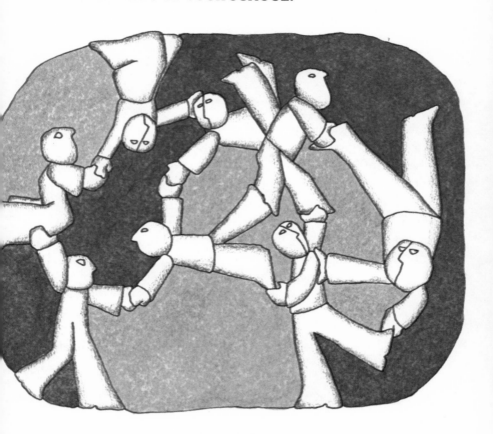

SUPPORTING EACH OTHER

When staff members are in positive contact and are communicating effectively, consideration may be given to developing systems within the school by which staff members can actively support each other. An effective school-support system does not have to be complex. It need only consist of behavior patterns developed by staff members to positively reinforce each other—behaviors stemming from a realization that "We are all in this together and no one can function properly unless all do."

One of the most successful ways of beginning to focus attention on the support concept is to introduce at a general staff meeting the questions, What is the most helpful thing that has ever been done for me by another staff member? and What kinds of things are done by school staff members for one another that make them feel worthwhile and cared for? Before answering these questions, the staff divides into small cross grade-level groups of five or six. Each small group then offers answers to the questions. Finally, all the small groups come together, and compile a master list of positive actions. You will find that the lists usually include items such as:

■ Inviting fellow teachers and classes to share special activities and experiences.

■ Taking on playground duties or other responsibilities for teachers who are not feeling well.

■ Helping fellow teachers in handling problems with students or parents.

■ Sharing materials and ideas with colleagues.

■ Helping teachers with clerical or menial tasks.

- Making teaching aids for each other.

- Interceding on behalf of a colleague with the principal, custodian, school secretary, or a parent.

- Taking responsibility for keeping colleagues informed when they miss meetings or other professional activities.

- Arranging for rap sessions or informal discussions of professional problems.

- Counseling each other on personal problems.

- Doing a personal kindness for a colleague during a time of trouble or stress.

- "Rescuing" a teacher who is trapped by an unreasonable or irate parent.

- Giving and graciously receiving sincere compliments on professional ability and personal qualities.

What the lists include is not nearly as important as the process of focusing on positive actions that teachers can take to help each other. ***Directing attention to such actions brings staff members to the realization that they have the power to support each other in ways that make school a better place for all.*** It also becomes apparent through this activity that most teachers do not consciously or actively move in these personal support directions in any type of organized manner.

Recognition and discussion of personal support actions may be directed toward obtaining a commitment from teachers to attempt to positively reinforce one or more teachers every day for a week. Nothing elaborate need be planned. The simple acts of reaching out to get to know someone they haven't had much contact with, by sharing materials or ideas, by planning a joint activity with a fellow teacher, or by engaging in any other involving activity should be purposefully attempted. At the next staff meeting, the week's actions may be discussed and evaluated. A positive difference in school climate is usually noted as a result of teachers' personal support efforts.

As teachers experience the payoff related to these actions in terms of more pleasant working conditions and professional improvement, they will continue to reach out toward one another. Formalized support-systems often develop as staffs begin to recognize that their cooperative power positively affects their professional environment. Some examples of support-systems which developed through such efforts are:

- Teachers teaming to teach in specific areas of strength.

- The development of peer-teaching and tutoring systems through the cooperation of primary and upper-grade teachers.

- Teacher development of simpler and more effective systems of reporting student progress to parents.

- Getting parents involved in a parents-aid-to-teachers program.

- Establishment of regular case-study meetings during which teachers pooled their resources in planning effective ways to help each other deal with students who had serious behavior or learning problems.

- Teacher development of methods and plans for dealing with high student transiency.

Formalized support-projects such as these are planned and carried out either by the total staff, by grade levels, by cross grade-

level planning-teams, or by ad hoc committees. These systems
differ in three important ways from the traditional administration or
school district initiated projects.

- ■ They originate at the grass-roots level as a result of a felt need
by local school personnel.

- ■ They result in more pleasant and rewarding working conditions.

- ■ They bring staff members into successful professional and
personal contact with each other.

As the payoffs are recognized, support-systems will continue to
improve and should in time lead to increased staff commitment
to involvement in and responsibility for the total school development.

**IN WHAT WAYS DO THE STAFF MEMBERS IN YOUR
SCHOOL SUPPORT EACH OTHER? HOW CAN THEY
IMPROVE THEIR SUPPORT OF EACH OTHER IN BOTH
PERSONAL AND PROFESSIONAL AREAS? ARE THEY
WILLING TO COMMIT THEMSELVES TO ACTION?**

**WHAT KINDS OF SYSTEMS CAN BE DEVELOPED IN
YOUR SCHOOL TO SAVE TEACHERS TIME AND EFFORT
AND TO MAKE WORKING CONDITIONS MORE
PLEASANT AND PROFESSIONALLY REWARDING?**

OPENING UP THE SCHOOL FOR TEACHERS

A climate of trust and mutual respect will not flourish in a
closed environment in which teachers keep their problems to
themselves and live out their professional lives in quiet desperation.
Some specific moves need to be made in the direction of reducing

the constraints of the average school environment. The following ideas are being used successfully in attempts to relieve the trapped and lonely feeling so often experienced by teachers.

■ Eliminate school bells. Bells are a source of irritation; they make teachers and students nervous; they hurt the ears and are useful and necessary only in case of emergency. All teachers and most students can tell time, so why not stop ringing bells on a trial basis and see what happens?

■ Co-mingle the classrooms in the school building. Place primary rooms among the upper-grade rooms so that the teachers and students can get to know and help each other. If there are special education classrooms in the school, mix them in with other rooms and avoid concentrating them in some remote corner.

■ Pair teachers on the buddy system. Pairing may be done on the basis of primary and upper-grade partners or on the basis of room partners. The idea is that each teacher has someone who cares. Each partner is responsible for the other in case of illness, absence, emergency, or special needs, such as obtaining important information or materials. Partners will also work together in relieving each other during inclement weather and at other times.

■ Arrange schedules so that teachers can see each other more often at noon and recess. Consider reducing the number of recesses and lunch periods in large schools so that as many teachers as possible can communicate at break times.

■ Enable classroom teachers to have spontaneous short breaks. Let administrators, counselors, nurses, or other auxiliary personnel relieve teachers occasionally once or twice a week for short periods of time. These breaks are usually welcome,

especially during the hectic times of the year and have a
positive effect on teacher morale.

■ Plan for interschool and intraschool visitations. Administrators
or other school staff members could cover classes and arrange
for combination programs in the auditorium, on the playground
or for having room partners cover for each other on a reciprocal
basis. Aides and parent volunteers may also be used to free
teachers. *One of the most professionally relevant and
productive activities that teachers can engage in is visiting
other classrooms or schools. This should be encouraged at
every opportunity, since it involves teachers positively with
one another.*

■ Temporarily team or combine classes for physical education,
music, or special auditorium programs. This is an easy way
for teachers to work with each other's classes, and it helps to
break the monotony of the self-contained classroom.

■ Invite parents and community members into the classroom
to talk with the students. Ask visitors to join students in a
discussion circle. Encourage parents and community leaders to
arrange trips for students and teachers into the local community.

■ Teachers make contingency plans to handle each other's
classes or to teach certain students within the classes on those
"difficult days." When tensions build, a change of scenery for
students and teachers is mutually beneficial.

These ideas may be tried and others may be developed by staff
members as they work to open up the school environment for
each other. Without purposeful and constructive attempts to reduce
loneliness imposed by the traditional egg-carton organization of
most schools, teachers will continue to feel trapped and confined,
and their feelings will hinder their professional effectiveness.

WHAT OPPORTUNITIES DO STAFF MEMBERS IN YOUR
SCHOOL HAVE FOR INTERACTING WITH EACH OTHER
DURING THE SCHOOL DAY? DO THEY OCCASIONALLY
WORK WITH EACH OTHER'S CLASSES? IN WHAT KINDS
OF COOPERATIVE ACTIVITIES DO THEY ENGAGE?

COULD YOUR STAFF DEVELOP SOME STRATEGIES IN
ADDITION TO THE ONES MENTIONED FOR THE
PURPOSE OF OPENING UP THE SCHOOL ENVIRONMENT?

THE ADMINISTRATOR'S ROLE IN DEVELOPING A CLIMATE OF TRUST

The personal and professional philosophy and style of the
local school principal has a profound effect on the human
environment of the school. What the principal does or does not
do will influence the quality of the interaction among other staff
members, teachers, students, and parents. If principals had
unlimited time, profound wisdom, irresistable charisma, boundless
energy, and the ability to walk on water, they might be able to
live up to some of the demands that are currently being made on
them. Unfortunately, they are merely human. They become tired,
lonely, and discouraged as do teachers, and therefore, they resent
much of the well-meaning advice that is offered by the experts.

In spite of the pressure, however, some principals act in ways
which lead to the development of warm, friendly, and positive
climates within their schools. But some do not. During fifteen
years as a school administrator, I learned more by observing and
talking with successful colleagues about what contributed to their

The principal has a profound effect on the human environment of the school.

success than I did by reading books on the subject. During the last two years, my scope of observation and conversation broadened considerably as I traveled to many school districts and had the opportunities to work with many extremely competent school administrators. An examination of the actions of those principals who seemed to promote a healthy climate of trust within their domains was most enlightening. I listed some of the factors that I observed. The following is not meant to be a cookbook of foolproof qualities, but rather ideas to be considered by those in school leadership positions.

Principals in positive climate schools:

■ model the actions that they wish to develop in their schools. Professor Arthur Lewis of Columbia University said, "Leaders in an organization get the kind of atmosphere they want—not the kind they say they want, but the kind they show they want by what they do."[19] This statement reinforces my observations. If principals expect teachers to be involved with students, the principals get involved with students, too. If they expect staff members to become close with each other, they are friendly and considerate in their relations with staff members. If they expect teachers to put in extra time on projects or with parents, principals put in extra time. Teachers, like students, learn by example more than by precept.

■ have credibility as educational leaders. Administrators who act as though the main business of the school were learning seem to be successful in developing positive school climates. They visit classrooms often. They hold discussions with students. They ask questions about teaching methods. They show interest

---

[19] Arthur J. Lewis, "The Future of the Elementary School Principalship," *The National Elementary Principal,* Sept. 1968, p. 14.

in new educational ideas and materials. They are visible in the school and are accessible to students, teachers, and parents.

■ have a realistic way of handling priorities. Students usually come first; teachers and parents come next; paper work finishes dead last. Principals who work this way handle the proliferating paper jam in the schools through creative delegation or benign neglect. Human problems always take priority over forms and inventories. Different ways of organizing time are developed by principals who have ESEA budgets and other demanding programs in order to get the job completed yet retain their credibility as educational leaders.

■ are personally or face-to-face oriented. Whether or not they have charisma, most principals of positive climate schools maintain continuous personal contact with their staff members. Not many days go by before any teacher on the staff has the opportunity to talk with the principal. These principals do more listening and talking than writing. If a message has to be delivered to a teacher, they usually walk to the classroom and deliver it orally, instead of using the mailbox. If a teacher asks for a conference, the principal often goes out to the teacher's classroom instead of holding it in his office. These principals also spend some time during lunch and recess in the teachers' lounge. Many problems in positive climate schools are solved during lunchtime. These leaders also tend to have close contact with fellow administrators and are not afraid to ask questions and share successes and failures with them.

■ are honest and fair with staff members. Teachers who work in positive climate schools are usually able to make statements about the principal, such as, I feel supported and I know where I stand. The principals do not play God or attempt to solve all problems, but they are willing to realistically present problems to the members of the staff and to involve them in appropriate decision-making processes.

■ are willing and able to delegate authority effectively. These principals know they can't do it all, but they are careful and skillful in delegating authority. They know their co-workers and do not give difficult jobs to people who can't handle them. They are competent in delegating authority, and they continually reinforce success.

■ are supportive of creative teachers. Creative ways of working with students—when carefully thought out—are enthusiastically supported and encouraged by principals of positive climate schools. These principals know how to ask the right questions to determine if ideas have true merit or are presented merely for the sake of change. Once it is established that new systems have value, they extend psychic and material support. This process of reinforcing creative and positive-thinking teachers seems far more successful than spending disproportionate amounts of time in attempting to upgrade apathetic or negative-thinking staff members.

■ are service oriented. These principals often ask their staff members how things are going. Teachers are surveyed, and their ideas and suggestions are acted upon. The principal regards himself more as a support person than as the traditional boss. He never stops thinking like a teacher, and he recognizes the importance of helping teachers obtain the materials, equipment, training, and time necessary for them to do their jobs effectively.

■ are community conscious. Successful principals develop the ability to bridge the gap between the school staff and the community. Making parents welcome and productive workers in the school without becoming a threat to teachers is a responsibility that these principals handle well. Community involvement in the schools is here to stay, and effective administrators are using this involvement in positive ways.

**IN WHAT WAYS DOES THE PRINCIPAL IN YOUR
SCHOOL ASSIST AND BECOME POSITIVELY INVOLVED
WITH THE STAFF MEMBERS?**

**IN WHAT WAYS DO STAFF MEMBERS IN YOUR
SCHOOL ASSIST AND BECOME POSITIVELY INVOLVED
WITH THE PRINCIPAL?**

**WHAT DO YOU THINK THE PRINCIPAL SHOULD DO TO
SUPPORT AND ASSIST THE STAFF IN ESTABLISHING
A POSITIVE SCHOOL CLIMATE?**

**WHAT DO YOU THINK THE STAFF SHOULD DO TO
SUPPORT AND ASSIST THE PRINCIPAL IN
ESTABLISHING A POSITIVE SCHOOL CLIMATE?**

A WORD TO THE DISTRICT OFFICE

I observe a direct correlation between the amount of contact school employees have with students and the credibility of those employees in the eyes of the community. For example, parents seem to place greater trust in teachers than in principals, in principals than in superintendents, and so on.

In attempts to bring parents and the school community closer together, many school districts are moving toward decentralization. Unfortunately, decentralization efforts place their major emphasis on the mechanical, managerial, and organizational functions of the district instead of on the improvement of the quality of personal contact between the district office and field personnel. I believe that unless the quality of this contact improves dramatically, many programs and systems initiated by school districts will fail in even greater numbers due to lack of interest and involvement on the part of field personnel.

If, however, district office personnel, such as consultants, specialists, supervisors, directors, and superintendents on various levels could arrange to spend a modest amount of their time in local schools *communicating with students in the classroom,* three important benefits would result.

■ Teachers and parents would feel less isolated and therefore more trusting of school personnel in policy-making positions.

■ Teachers and principals would feel that their work in the classrooms is important and worthwhile. Reinforcement of local school efforts by the physical presence of district office personnel is far more powerful than the traditional letters, bulletins or mass meetings.

■ District office personnel would gain valuable insights into the specific problems schools face each day and would also increase their educational credibility with local school people.

Although it would be unrealistic to suggest that superintendents spend large amounts of time in the school, I nonetheless feel that a reordering of priorities could allow more time for upper-echelon administrators and their staffs to have more frequent contact with students, teachers, and principals. My experience and observation of districts in which attempts are made to establish such contacts indicate that the resulting improvement of morale make it well worth the effort.

HOW OFTEN DO YOU SEE NONADMINISTRATIVE
DISTRICT OFFICE STAFF MEMBERS OR
ADMINISTRATORS ABOVE THE LEVEL OF PRINCIPAL
IN YOUR SCHOOL?

DO DISTRICT OFFICE PERSONNEL EVER COME INTO
THE CLASSROOMS AND CONDUCT SERIOUS AND
MEANINGFUL DISCUSSIONS WITH STUDENTS? IF NOT,
HOW COULD SUCH VISITATION BE ENCOURAGED?

A NOTE ABOUT PARENT INVOLVEMENT

Most parents want their children to attend school in a pleasant and friendly environment in which they will work with teachers who care about them and in which they will learn necessary skills and gain knowledge. When children aren't successful in school, many parents become frustrated and are at a loss as to what to do. Their reactions vary.

Resigned Parent: "It's no use going down there. The principal protects the teacher, and you don't get anywhere."

Unconcerned Parent: "It's my kid's problem. He'll have to work it out for himself."

Hostile Parent; "I'm going down there and rattle some cages. By God they'll know I've been there!"

All of these reactions are dead ends in terms of helping the student, since they serve only to feed antagonisms and increase personal separation.

In spite of the desire of teachers and administrators for positive parent involvement and the desire of parents for positive contact with teachers and principals, the alienation within the school often carries over into relationships among parents and school personnel.

When there is little consistency among teachers in the way they work with parents, comparisons are inevitable. Three or four teachers in a given school can enjoy an excellent reputation in the community because they write notes home and confer with parents frequently. They might send special work home with students and follow-through with telephone calls or home visits. Other teachers in the school might resent these "average raisers," and divisiveness may develop and grow within the staff. Although parents may become aware of internal school problems, there is very little that they can do about it. It is up to the faculty to handle such problems by working together toward achieving a consensus regarding parent-school communications. *There is, however, a very definite and positive role which a parent can play in helping schools develop friendlier, less isolating, and more effective learning environments.* This role is becoming clearer as demands for local control and involvement in the school are increasing. Although it is impossible to examine in this book the enormous problem of school-community relations, a few suggestions are offered for parents who wish to help reduce home-school separation.

- Visit your child's teacher *before* problems develop. Always try to reinforce something positive that the teacher has done or is doing for your child. Remember that teacher efforts usually increase when parents show positive nonthreatening interest.

- Ask your child's teacher or principal about the separators in this book that concern you. Ask what you can do to help make school a friendlier place for students and teachers.

- Help your child plan *specific* ways of becoming positively involved with his teacher. Discuss with your child how he approaches and talks with his teacher, where he sits in class, what to do when he has a problem while the teacher is busy, and other nitty-gritty items which relate to teacher-student contact.

- Join and regularly attend meetings of your local PTA and/or Parent-Community Advisory Group, if your school has one.

- Form an *active* parent education committee, if none exists. Focus efforts on important issues, such as responsible student behavior, student learning patterns, teacher accountability, and community-school involvement.

- Suggest the initiation of professional/social community meetings at which parents and teachers can begin to establish contact. Invite teachers and administrators to meet with parents in homes, schools and churches in the community for the purpose of discussing educational goals and activities.

- Offer your services as a volunteer or an aide in assisting teachers in the preparation of teaching materials or in working with students.

- Use this book individually or with other parents to help you view the school through the eyes of the students, teachers, and administrators. Use it as a guide for evaluating the quality of the environment in which your child is learning.

Many parents will be reluctant to take some of these steps and will be apprehensive about approaching the authority-laden school with any kind of concern or suggestion. Some may even feel physical discomfort associated with their own past experiences as a student. Some grown men tell me that the sights, sounds, and smells of a school make them very uneasy. Historically, school people contributed to these feelings by making parents feel neither welcome nor worthwhile. Fortunately, this situation is changing as perceptive teachers and administrators become increasingly aware that positive parent support is essential to the survival of effective educational programs.

My advice is to reach out, and if you are not already positively involved with your local school, try some of the suggestions offered and see what happens.

IN WHAT ADDITIONAL WAYS CAN PARENTS AND TEACHERS COOPERATE IN MAKING THE SCHOOL A FRIENDLIER AND LESS LONELY PLACE?

How can parents and school staff members arrange to meet for the purpose of improving the school's learning environment? How can existing community resources be used in this task?

CONCLUSION

Identifying and treating the specific conditions that make adults and students in the schools feel lonely is an essential first step toward improving education. In these pages I have described certain kinds of loneliness-causing factors, and I have offered some field-tested suggestions for correcting them. The ideas and activities included in this book are working effectively in the schools for which they were planned. They cannot be applied mechanically since each school staff is unique. Therefore, each staff must develop its own system for dealing with particular problems in their school.

If the people in your school are interested in achieving greater professional satisfaction and a more effective learning environment, they can begin the process of change by:

■ Discussing the quality of life in the school and making a group commitment to improve it.

■ Reviewing this book together.

■ Using the planning sheets in Part I.

■ Discussing the questions in Part II and taking subsequent action that is relevant to the school.

■ Using the selected references as resource material.

Loneliness and fears of inadequacy will be reduced in direct proportion to the efforts of teachers and administrators in meeting and planning together to create a climate of trust and caring. This small book identifies issues, asks questions, and proposes action. Realistically, that is all a book can do—the rest is up to the reader.

SELECTED REFERENCES

The following publications have been invaluable to me as sources of ideas for building more rewarding and productive human relationships in schools. Since most teachers and principals are too busy to go through volumes of material in search of a few useful suggestions, this list is short and is very briefly annotated.

Ashton-Warner, Sylvia. *Teacher.* New York: Simon and Schuster,Inc., 1963. (Education based on true involvement between teacher and young child, plus practical suggestions for teaching experience-centered reading and writing.)

Dreikurs, Rudolf. *Psychology In the Classroom.* New York: Harper & Row, 1957. (Practical ways of achieving nonpunitive and nonpermissive discipline in school. An alternative to punishment, the emphasis is on natural and logical consequences.)

Ginott, Haim. *Teacher and Child.* New York: Macmillan & Co., 1972. (Filled with suggestions to facilitate teacher-student communication. Specific ways to help improve the quality of life within the classroom are included.)

Glasser, William. *Reality Therapy.* New York: Harper & Row, 1965. (A basic common sense approach for helping people who have difficulty in responsibly meeting their basic needs for love and self-worth.)

Glasser, William. *Schools Without Failure.* New York: Harper & Row, 1969. (Applies William Glasser's theories of Reality Therapy to contemporary educational problems. Special emphasis is placed on class discussion meetings and the prevention of school failure through involvement, relevance and thinking.)

Greer, Mary, and Rubinstein, Bonnie. *Will the Real Teacher Please Stand Up.* Pacific Palisades, California: Goodyear Publishing Co., 1972. (A primer in humanistic education. Filled with helpful and practical ideas, from many sources, aimed at helping students and teachers become effectively involved with learning by becoming more effectively involved with each other.)

Group for Environment Education Inc. *Yellow Pages of Learning Resources.* Cambridge, Massachusetts: The MIT Press, 1972. (An excellent source book for relevant learning, which if used according to directions should bring teachers and students closer together through shared learning experiences.)

Holt, John. *How Children Fail.* New York: Pitman Publishing Co., 1964. (A strong indictment of most current educational systems. Useful in helping to recognize the strategies developed by children to protect themselves from failure-promoting school practices.)

Postman, Neil, and Weingartner, Charles. *Teaching As a Subversive Activity.* New York: Delacorte Press, 1969. (Alternatives to current alienating classroom practices. Specific suggestions for bringing meaning to the classroom so that students can experience learning based on success.)

Silberman, Charles. *Crisis In The Classroom.* New York: Random House, 1970. (A comprehensive and scholarly study of what is wrong with our schools and what to do about it.)

NOTES

NOTES

NOTES

NOTES

NOTES

NOTES

NOTES

NOTES

NOTES

NOTES

NOTES